UNITY

The Creative Foundation of

PEACE

UNITY
The Creative Foundation of
PEACE

H. B. Danesh, M.D.

Bahá'í Studies Publications, Ottawa/Fitzhenry-Whiteside, Toronto

Bahá'í Studies Publications, Ottawa, Canada
Fitzhenry-Whiteside, Toronto, Canada

© 1986 by Hossain B. Danesh, M.D.

Published 1986. Revised Edition 1986
Printed in Canada

91 90 89 88 87 86   5 4 3 2 1

ISBN 0-920904-14-9

To

Shoghi Effendi

*whose penetrating insight, remarkable vision, and unique leadership
have made signal contributions to the cause of world peace*

Grammatical Note

The English language does not always permit reference to human beings without gender identification. In writing this book, the author has attempted, wherever possible, to avoid such bias. However, the reader should be assured that whenever the words, "man," "mankind," and "he/his" are used, the reference is to all members of humanity, without respect to gender.

Contents

Contents

Preface

In November 1984, I had the honour of presenting a talk at the Peace and New World Order session of the Ninth Annual Conference of the Association for Bahá'í Studies. The title of this talk was "Unity: The Creative Foundation of Peace." Since then, I have had the opportunity to expand greatly the scope of my study and research on peace and related issues, such as the psychosocial theories of human violence, Bahá'í perspectives on human society and its development, new approaches for the management and prevention of violence, and finally, models for the creation of a new world order.

From the beginning, my objective was to put forward, to the best of my ability, a comprehensive and integrated formulation about peace and its prerequisites. Very soon in my work I realized that the quest for peace was not enough and that to achieve peace we first have to create a condition of unity. Furthermore, my studies showed that the greater the degree and the broader the scope of unity, the greater the degree and scope of peace which results. It also became apparent to me that while the prerequisite for peace is unity, the prerequisite for unity is maturity—and maturity is an inevitable law of life. Following this line of reasoning, it is clear that world peace is indeed inevitable, and that our task is to hasten and facilitate the advent of peace by consciously focussing our attention on its prerequisites and dynamics.

This book is the result of these efforts, and its completion is to a very large degree due to the assistance, patience, and insight of many remarkable individuals. It would be difficult to mention every one of them here, but I wish to name at least a few. Any undertaking of this nature is not only enriching, but also extremely time-consuming. Consequently, in being able to write this book I feel a deep sense of gratitude to the members of my family, my wife Michele and our sons Arman and Roshan, who through their love, patience, and wisdom made it possible for me to invest all the time and energy the book required. Christine Zerbinis, Peter Morgan, Nancy Ackerman, and Ann Boyles read the manuscript and offered valuable suggestions for the development of its contents and style. Furthermore, Christine Zerbinis and Ann Boyles spent innumerable hours editing the manuscript and refining it for publication. Patricia Murray, Shelly Adams, and Carmel Hatcher helped type and wordprocess the various drafts; Wynne Morgan assisted in proofreading the book; Stephen Gouthro and Betty Butterill prepared the index; and Stan Phillips contributed his talents in the design of the book. My profound thanks go to each and every one of them. Undertakings of this nature are seldom the fruits of the work of a single individual, and in this case it is most assuredly the fruit of the united and generous efforts of many.

Toronto
April 1986

Part One:

Quest for Peace

1

The Eternal Quest for Peace:
An Introduction

They shall beat their swords into plowshares, and their spears into pruning hooks: nation shall not lift up sword against nation, neither shall they learn war anymore.
— Isaiah 2:4

The wish for peace has always occupied a place in the minds and hearts of people. The history of mankind, however, is filled with accounts of competition, rivalry, and war, as nations celebrate the lives of their war heroes, recount their national victories, and pride themselves on their ability to defeat other armies and kill or imprison enemies. History is also rife with contradictory documentation of the reasons various wars have been waged, rationalizing unimaginable degrees of pain, misery, grief, and the death of untold multitudes. Paradoxically, such acts of destruction and violence are often justified in the name of justice, equality, progress, religion, love of one's people, and love of God.

The history of the nations of the world is written according to the precepts of competition and the doctrines of supremacy and dominance. We would be hard pressed to find a nation willing to express its history according to the principles of universal brotherhood, true equality, and the nobility of all men and women. Such a rendition of history would require courage and insight, characteristics of a truly mature and civilized people, the likes of which mankind has not yet witnessed. Chronicling history from the perspective of the powerful and life-generating forces of peace would allow us to develop new insights into the motives behind war and, more important, into the conditions necessary to create peace. While the history of nations focusses on wars, triumphs, and defeats, the deeply-felt quest of their peoples (as depicted in their literature, poetry, music, art, and spiritual strivings) is toward love, peace, and unity.

War causes more than separation, doubt, and death. It is also responsible for much fear, helplessness, and hopelessness. Natalya Reshetovskaya, wife of Aleksandr Solzhenitsyn, wrote the following to her husband while he was in the army during the Second World War:

> My dearest!
> Where are you?
> We will probably stop for a while in Alma-Ata.
> What happens next no one knows. I live in the hope that you will eventually find me. . . .[1]

For her, there was some hope in the midst of war, but for the Indians at Wounded Knee there was none:

> There was no hope on earth, and God seemed to have forgotten us. Some said they saw the Son of God; others did not see Him. If He had come, He would do some great things as He had done before. We doubted it because we had seen neither Him nor His works. The people did not know; they did not care. . . .They screamed like crazy men to Him for mercy. They caught at the promise they heard He had made. The white men were frightened and called for soldiers. We had begged for life, and the white men thought we wanted theirs. We heard that soldiers were coming.[2]

Similarly, Tolstoy saw fear, the profound fear that takes over people during war — fear not only of being killed, but also of being tempted to kill and of actually killing another human being:

> Rostov was still pondering on his brilliant exploit, which, to his amazement, had won him the St. George's Cross and made his reputation indeed for fearless gallantry. There was something he could not fathom in it. "So they are even more frightened than

4

we are," he thought. "Why, is this all that's meant by heroism? And did I do it for the sake of my country? And was he to blame with his dimple and his blue eyes? How frightened he was! He thought I was going to kill him. Why should I kill him? My hand trembled. And they have given me the St. George's Cross. I can't make it out, I can't make it out!"[3]

The hopelessness, fear, and destruction caused by war is so immense that prevention of war, particularly in our world today, emerges as the greatest need of humanity. But prevention of war is in itself not sufficient.

The challenge before us, at this juncture in our collective history, is to create a world society, united in its objectives and aspirations, that will provide each individual and all nations with a well-founded security, true freedom and liberty, unqualified justice and equality. By taking on this task, we can end an era of fascination with war and initiate an age of "most great peace":

> These fruitless strifes, these ruinous wars shall pass away, and the "Most Great Peace" shall come. . . .These strifes and this bloodshed and discord must cease, and all men be as one kindred and one family. . . .Soon will the present-day order be rolled up, and a new one spread out in its stead.[4]

There is no doubt that the present-day order has proven inadequate to meet the current needs of humanity. It is also clear that mankind has become increasingly confused about the causes of war and impotent to prevent conflict. Club of Rome members Aurelio Peccei and Alexander King state:

> Modern man, despite the wonderful body of knowledge and information that he has accumulated and the means to apply it, appears to be muddling ahead as if he were blind or drugged, staggering from one crisis to another. It is increasingly evident that he is unsure of where he is going or where he wants to go beyond the next few tentative steps.[5]

This book attempts to clarify some of the more important reasons for mankind's failure to eradicate war and establish peace. Beginning with a focus on the present condition of mankind—its quest for peace, dependence on war, the violence committed in the name of love, and the awakening to the concept of world peace—the book then addresses the fundamental conceptual issue that peace cannot be pursued in and of itself.

5

Like happiness, peace is a state achieved when certain conditions are created, and since the prerequisite of peace is unity, it is unity which we must pursue.

This unity must be so broad that it will include all the nations and countries of the world, and yet be so specific that it will not exclude any individual from its unconditional acceptance of people as equal, noble, and unique. The achievement of such universal unity requires a change in our mind-set, in our daily behaviour vis-à-vis the issues of power and love in interpersonal relationships, in our understanding of and approach to freedom, in our use of science and technology, and in our perception of reality. The book proposes to study these issues from the perspective of practical steps that we, individually and collectively, can take as our contribution to the goal of establishing a new world order, the dominant feature of which must be peace. The third part of the book focusses on some of the characteristics of a new world order to be established. Violence is examined as a symptom of the greater problem of disunity rather than as a phenomenon in itself. A new way of dealing with violence is described, an approach which transcends both the aggressive attack and the nonviolent resistance methods of dealing with violence and uses the life-engendering powers of love and growth to counter human violence and destruction. Finally, the book examines the experience of the Bahá'í community as a prototype of this response and advances the "politics of transformation" for a world moving toward the unity paradigm.

2

A Look at the Present: From Separation to Unity

How long will humanity persist in its waywardness?
How long will injustice continue?
How long is chaos and confusion to reign amongst men?
How long will discord agitate the face of society?
The winds of despair are, alas, blowing from every direction, and the
strifes that divideth and afflicteth the human race are daily increasing.
The signs of impending convulsion and chaos can now be discerned,
inasmuch as the prevailing order appeareth to be lamentably
defective. . . .
　　　—Bahá'u'lláh

At this time more than any other in history, the leaders and thoughtful citizens of the world are aware of the need for peace. At least three conditions distinguish the present from the past in increasing this awareness. Most important is the phenomenal increase in the destructive capacity of humanity; mankind has never been so capable of or so close to total self-destruction. The second reason for this heightened awareness is the astonishing progress that has taken place in the fields of communication, transportation, and information exchange. These developments have simultaneously increased and decreased the threat of war. On the one hand, little time is needed to begin a war over a situation of misunderstanding or mistrust between two or more nations, while on the other hand, equally little time is needed to clarify the misunderstanding and resolve the mistrust, if the will to do so is present. The third reason for people's improved awareness of peace is the increased willingness of ordinary citizens in every country and from many diverse backgrounds to contribute, even sacrificially, to the efforts aimed at establishing a meaningful and lasting world peace.

These hopeful signs are, however, countered by the fact that, in our world today, there are still many wars waged, and a shaky, limited peace is barely maintained through the forces of fear and threat. Furthermore, violence of all kinds has become common and is often committed in the name of love and brotherhood.

If we are truly to appreciate our precarious condition in respect to the achievement of peace, we need to approach the challenge from totally new perspectives and with very different solutions. These solutions should open the way for contributions from every individual, family, group, and nation in the world and should take full advantage of the enormous creative capacity of humanity. To formulate such a comprehensive approach, we need first to review our present circumstances, which we will do by looking at the current situation in respect to peace, the alarming prevalence of violence, and, finally, the emerging world awareness about the need for peace.

Peace at Gunpoint

More than an end to war, we want an end to the beginnings of all wars.
—Franklin D. Roosevelt

Two commonly-accepted definitions of peace are a state of mental or physical quiet, tranquillity, and calm; and freedom from war or civil strife. According to these definitions, the world of humanity has never experienced a state of complete peace. Today, the minds of people are agitated, with anxiety and fear prevailing in the lives of many, and anger and distrust pervading the world. A state of tranquillity is difficult to find. Likewise, the other definition of peace, "freedom from war or civil strife," exists only to a limited degree and only in some parts of the world. Janez Stanovnik, the Executive Secretary of the United Nations Economic Commission for Europe, noted in 1978 that "since the Second World War, 199 wars have been fought in the world, 350 years have been spent on fighting them, . . . 69 countries have been directly the theatre of a war, and. . .no fewer than 81 countries have been directly or indirectly involved in these war conflicts since 1945."[1] These statistics have, alas, greatly increased since that statement.

Even in those regions and countries where there exists a condition of freedom from war and civil strife, the primary preoccupation of the governments is to increase armaments and military power and, concurrently, to find the means of creating a society less threatened by war. Although in these countries the tanks are not roaring and the missiles are not fired, they are nevertheless in a state of readiness and aimed at their intended targets. Thus, our present condition is that of readiness for war, which can hardly be described as a condition of peace.

Over half a century ago, before both the First and Second World Wars, 'Abdu'l-Bahá observed

> . . .that the most advanced and civilized countries of the world have been turned into arsenals of explosives, that the continents of the globe have been transformed into huge camps and battlefields, and that the peoples of the world have formed themselves into armed nations and that the governments of the world are vying with each other as to who will first step into the field of carnage and bloodshed, thus subjecting mankind to the utmost degree of affliction.[2]

Some sixty years and two world wars later, humanity is poised at the brink of yet another holocaust, one that can potentially destroy the human race.

It is rather puzzling that humanity has not learned from the experiences of the First and Second World Wars, continuing to behave as it had in the past. A look at the contemporary world shows that several factors of a psychological, socioeconomic, and spiritual nature play a role in the maintenance of an atmosphere of hostility and war.

The most obvious and important psychological causes are fear, suspicion, and anger. The world today is divided into a number of groups opposed along ideological, racial, religious, and economic lines, each seemingly fearful, suspicious, and hostile toward the others and attempting

9

to gain an upper hand in their competitive struggle. Added to this situation is humanity's history and present record of injustice, inequality, colonialism, and cruel dominance, the reality and memory of which are kept alive so that a consuming fire of hatred and mistrust is constantly fuelled by those who were and are its victims. Children are indoctrinated with a view of a world inhabited by dangerous, inferior, violent, undesirable, strange, and evil "others," who should be avoided, dominated, controlled and, if necessary, annihilated. Consequently, every new generation is raised with more fear, suspicion, and anger and provided with more deadly weapons as people continue their competitive war against compatriots who merely happen to live in another part of the world, belong to a different race of people, speak a different language, worship in a unique manner, or organize and govern their society in a particular way. However, psychological causes of war are preventable. With a program of universal education based on the principles of the oneness of mankind, new generations can be raised to see the "world [as] but one country, and mankind its citizens."[3]

The socioeconomic causes of war are based on the injustice and inequality which exist among the people as well as the nations of the world in respect to wealth and material and social well-being. Wealth and the possession of goods and material resources make their possessors stronger than those who are lacking, and this phenomenon is especially apparent in a world where mistrust and competition are prevalent. In the world today we observe an immense economic rivalry between the capitalistic and Marxist-communist nations, a rivalry which has resulted in the division of the world into two armed camps, each ready to prove to the other the supremacy of its economic system by demonstrating the greater destructiveness of its war machines. One is thus forced to conclude that the present dominant economic ideologies have contributed much more to the creation of injustice, inequality, and war than to the cause of justice, equality, and peace. As Fritjof Capra notes: "Today's world economy is based on past configurations of power, perpetuating class structures and unequal distribution of wealth within national economies, as well as exploitation of Third World countries by rich industrialized nations."[4] Such conditions of injustice and inequality are fertile grounds for upheavals, revolutions, and wars.

Finally, the spiritual cause of war is the most crucial issue. One could, with much assurance, contend that at the root of all human wars lies a spiritual disease—misguided value systems, self-centredness, disregard for man's noble nature, and an ignorance of the purpose of the life of humanity—all spiritual issues largely ignored in the world today and whose absence has greatly contributed to the prevalence of war. Shoghi Effendi, in a letter addressed to Dr. Stanwood Cobb, dated October 18, 1948, wrote:

> You should guard against one impression . . . and that is that the worst is over, humanity out of the woods, and millennium just around the corner! It is becoming increasingly obvious that the world crisis is not yet over, and may not yet have reached its highest point. People must be made to realize that until they learn the true nature of man, and abide by the spiritual laws governing him, the convulsions, the economic and political strife torturing the world, the immorality, will not get better, but will go on until out of the ashes—if necessary—the phoenix of the New World will rise.

The psychological, socioeconomic, and spiritual causes of war all have one thing in common: they separate people from each other, cause distance and disunity, create strangeness and inequality, and justify human violence by ignoring or denying the nobility of all people. Therefore, by their disunifying nature, they prevent the creation of a truly peaceful world, and this leads to an important observation concerning our world today: The world climate is not yet appropriate for the growth of peace.

In order to create a climate in which peace will have a chance to grow, we need to reexamine our views about human violence and love, as well as the relationship of each to the other and to peace. Such an examination, both from a scientific and historical perspective, will show that many current difficulties in respect to these issues have their roots in our misguided and baseless conceptions about the nature and the relationship of violence, love, and peace.

Violence in the Name of Love

I love her and she loves me, and we hate each other with a
wild hatred born of love.
  —H.L. Mencken

Accompanying the alarming stance of world governments towards the use of violence in the name of peace is the appalling prevalence of violence at

11

the interpersonal level, in the name of love. Many people commit acts of violence because of love for country, religion, race, tribe, or family. Many leaders, in their quest for supremacy, power, and control, instil in their subjects fear and hatred of their so-called enemies, those who are members of a different race or who speak another language, belong to different religions, or are different in one way or another. These feelings of fear and hatred are ultimately expressed in the form of violence and war, all practiced in the name of love and security.

Likewise, it is a fact that most crimes take place between people who "love" each other. The majority of murders in the United States are committed in the home by people who know each other. Crimes of passion, murders committed for the sake of love, and the high incidence of child and wife abuse are just a few examples of the prevalence of violence in the context of love relationships.[5]

On October 24, 1912, while in Paris speaking about the need for a universal and unlimited love, 'Abdu'l-Bahá reviewed the various types of love and pointed out that some types, by nature of their limited scope, cause disunity and disharmony between people. He said:

> The perfect love needs an unselfish instrument, absolutely freed from fetters of every kind. The love of family is limited; the tie of blood relationship is not the strongest bond. Frequently members of the same family disagree, and even hate each other.
>
> Patriotic love is finite; the love of one's country causing hatred of all others, is not perfect love! Compatriots also are not free from quarrels amongst themselves. The love of race is limited; there is some union here, but that is insufficient. Love must be free from boundaries!
>
> To love our own race may mean hatred of all others, and even people of the same race often dislike each other.
>
> Political love also is much bound up with hatred of one party for another; this love is very limited and uncertain.
>
> The love of community of interest in service is likewise fluctuating; frequently competitions arise, which lead to jealousy, and at length hatred replaces love. . . .All these ties of love are imperfect. It is clear that limited material ties are insufficient to adequately express the universal love. . . .[6]

In order to achieve the universal love called for by 'Abdu'l-Bahá, we need to reexamine our views on love and its relation to violence. The currently dominant psychological formulations consider love and aggression (and violence) to be closely linked. Freud, for example, believed that both aggression and love exist in man; however, the former is much more powerful than the latter and, consequently, the forces of love in man are not infrequently defeated by the forces of aggression.[7]

Konrad Lorenz, however, sees love and aggression as totally interdependent. With his ideas coming from the study of animals and man, he observes, "A personal bond. . .is found only in animals with highly developed intra-specific aggression, in fact this bond is the firmer, the more aggressive the particular animal and species is."[8] In these animals, the existence of a bond similar to human love, according to Lorenz, is dependent on the existence of a high level of aggression, and thus, from this perspective, it is not possible to love without aggression and violence. Lorenz believes that the same principles apply to man.

In his critique on the work of Lorenz, Ashley Montagu points out that "arguments based on fish, birds, and other animals are strictly for them. They have no relevance for man."[9] Montagu further observes:

> Everything points to the nonviolence of the greater part of early man's life, to the contribution made by the increasing development of cooperative activities, the very social process of hunting itself, the invention of speech, the development of food-getting and food-preparing tools, and the like.[10]

These conclusions are supported by the work of Richard Leakey. In the book, *Origins*, which Leakey wrote in collaboration with Roger Lewin, science editor of *New Scientist*, the following question is posed: ". . .why is it that humanity seems determined to spiral ever faster towards self-made destruction?"[11] The authors then go on to reject arguments put forward by researchers and writers such as Raymond Dart, Konrad Lorenz, and Robert Audrey. In part, Leakey and Lewin say:

> The core of the aggression argument says that because we share a common heritage with the animal kingdom we must possess and express an aggressive instinct. And the notion is elaborated with the suggestion that at some point in our evolutionary history we gave up being vegetarian ape-like creatures and became killers, with a taste not only for prey animals but also for each other. It makes a good gripping story. More important, it

absolves society from attempting to rectify the evil in the world. But it is fiction—dangerous fiction. . . .Indeed, we argue that the opposite is true, that humans could not have evolved in the remarkable way in which we undoubtedly have unless our ancestors were strongly cooperative creatures.[12]

Elsewhere, I have shown that human aggression is an unhealthy response to the life processes of threats and opportunities.[13] At any given time, we face threats of a varied nature: physical, in the form of disease and hunger; psychological, in the form of rejection, loss, abandonment, or humiliation, domination, and manipulation; and spiritual threats, such as lack of a purpose in life. When threatened, we respond with feelings of anger, fear, and anxiety, and if unable, for whatever reason, to deal with these feelings, we may resort to aggression and violence.

In addition to threats, we are also constantly offered opportunities to grow and to create. Growth and creativity are both uniquely human capacities that depend on the nurturing qualities of love and encouragement. An individual who receives encouragement and love in his efforts to grow and create is able to achieve a considerable degree of maturity and fulfillment. Conversely, in the absence of love and encouragement the individual remains immature, unsure of himself, bored, and unfulfilled in his life. These conditions threaten the individual and may eventually lead him to destructive forms of behaviour aimed either at self, in the form of apathy and depression, or at others, in the form of aggression and violence.

From the foregoing perspectives on human aggression and violence, we reach two conclusions. First, human violence cannot be explained—let alone justified—by animal studies, theories of evolution, and psychological or social explanations, alone or combined. Human aggression can be understood and explained only when the spiritual aspects of human reality are taken into account and their relationship with and effects on other dimensions of human reality are understood and integrated. Second, although love and aggression are interconnected at the early levels of individual and collective growth, in the course of their evolution they travel very different routes. While aggression peaks sometime during adolescence or early adulthood and then begins a downward process which is never reversed, love evolves in an upward process which has no limit.

There are several reasons for the confusion and vagueness that surround the issue of human love. Many see love as a weakness, illness, or neurosis: Robert Burton describes love as a "disease, frenzy" and "hell";

William James connects love with sexual impulse, as does Freud. In fact, most modern works on love relate love to "libido," the sexual instinctual drive existing in both man and animals. According to this view, love is strongest when sexual impulses are allowed to be fully satisfied.[14] One of the advocates of this perspective on love is philosopher Arno Plack, who believes that all evil in society is due to the suppression of our basic drives, particularly our sexual drive. Plack believes that "it is impossible for a person to be contented, peaceable and at the same time sexually dissatisfied. To demand humility, love of one's fellow man and renunciation of the basic drives from one and the same person is to demand too much of him, both of his morals and of his nerves."[15]

Other theories consider love as a neurosis, as a projection of competition with one's father, as "anti-social" behaviour, and as a condition which includes suffering and death and, therefore, is contrary to the forces of life. Kenneth Pope differentiates between human love in general, such as "love of country, of God, of activities, or of things," and romantic love which, for him, is the main type of love between two individuals, usually, but not exclusively, members of the opposite sex.[16]

There is, however, another view of love: as the very source of life, of togetherness, cooperation, unity, growth, development, and exaltation. 'Abdu'l-Bahá declares that "love is the cause of the existence of all phenomena and the absence of love is the cause of disintegration or non-existence." After describing other important aspects of love, 'Abdu'l-Bahá concludes: "It is therefore evident that in the world of humanity the greatest king and sovereign is love. If love were extinguished, the power of attraction dispelled, the affinity of human hearts destroyed, the phenomena of human life would disappear."[17]

These divergent views clearly show that we need to develop a comprehensive and coherent perspective on love, towards which goal I advance a number of ideas.

To love is a normal human attribute. There exists in man a motivating force which impels him to seek knowledge, to search for truth, to behold beauty, to experience the most, to reach the highest, to create the best and, above all, to achieve a union with his beloved. These fundamental quests are the manifestations of the basic and eternal love inherent in every human being.

At its most primitive level, love manifests itself in the form of biological needs and desires of newly-born infants. At this stage, we are totally self-centred. However, we soon become aware of others in our life and begin a process of social interaction characterized by the display of excitement, satisfaction, and enjoyment—responses which form the foundation of a love relationship between us and our parents and eventually between us and the world. Love at this level, therefore, is a combination of at least four components: our experiential awareness of our own basic biological needs and desires; our enjoyment, satisfaction, and excitement in response to the gratification of these needs and desires; our ability to trust those who are responsible for our care; and an awareness, however dim, of the fact that communication of these feelings further enhances these pleasurable experiences.

As we grow and mature, our desires gradually broaden in scope and become more specific in application. As young people, we choose objects of desire and pay them special attention. Interest in physical activities, artistic endeavours, scientific learning, and material acquisition are some of the more specific manifestations of our general desire. However, in addition, we also focus our strivings, desires, and quests on other people, especially on our parents, siblings, family members, friends, and teachers. Eventually, under ordinary circumstances, one individual becomes the focal point of our love, and we establish a very close emotional bond. At this point marriage becomes a possibility and hence, given the universality of this process, marriage exists in all cultures.

Beyond love in marriage, however, we continue our quest for truth and beauty and are never totally satisfied in this respect. This developmental process, through which primitive and dimly understood desires give way to a striving for excellence and a quest for the Ultimate, eventually evolves into human love of the Absolute and the Eternal.

At least two factors influence evolution of human love: the individual's conscious awareness of the nature of love and the chosen love object. In order for our capacity in this area to be used in a mature way, we must become aware of the developmental nature of love and identify those factors which hamper its growth. Love, like any other human quality, begins in a state of potentiality. Actualization of this potential, however, depends on our deliberate efforts to increase our awareness of the prerequisites for the growth of our love, and on the type of love object that we choose for ourselves. These factors are of considerable importance.

To love is natural to all people, but who, what, and how we love determine the quality and the nature of our love. If we love with passion and sensuality alone, our attention will focus solely on the physical characteristics of our beloved. If we choose to make scientific knowledge our primary love object, then our time, energy, and activities will be basically devoted to the pursuit of objectives and activities which make the acquisition of science easier for us. If we choose a limited and temporary love object, our love will likewise be limited and temporary. Conversely, if our love object is meaningful and universal, our love will also be more profound and all-encompassing, and so there is a direct relationship between who and what we love and the kind of love we experience.

In the final analysis, enlightened and mature human love is the cause of growth and development in both the individual and the society and is an effective antidote for human aggression. Such love greatly facilitates humanity's march away from aggression and violence and assures arrival at the city of unity. Unity and peace are closely related and their importance in shaping the fortunes of humanity is gaining significance for people everywhere. Such awareness ultimately needs to be translated into coherent and comprehensive concepts and specific strategies to establish world peace.

The Emerging Awareness of Peace

Will it come, or will it not,
The day when the joy becomes great
The day when the grief becomes small?
 —Gunar Ekelof

The contemporary situation in respect to peace is not completely negative. There is, at present, an emerging worldwide awareness of the critical conditions of our time, reflected by the extremely volatile atmosphere of conflict and animosity between major military powers and economic blocs, as well as the ever-present threat of a nuclear conflict that could result in the annihilation of the whole human race.

This awareness is manifested in the organization of many groups dedicated to the cause of peace and the prevention of war. These groups, through a variety of methods and in an increasingly effective manner, are helping to create an atmosphere where peace is attractive and war is viewed with abhorrence. Historical and social studies indicate that when a critical number of individuals in a society develop a new perspective on a given issue, their awareness puts into motion the mechanism necessary for change. As Toynbee observes:

17

During the disintegration of a civilization, two separate plays with different plots are being performed simultaneously side by side. While an unchanging dominant majority is perpetually rehearsing its own defeat, fresh challenges are perpetually evoking fresh creative responses from newly recruited minorities, which proclaim their own creative power by rising, each time, to the occasion. The drama of challenge-and-response continues to be performed, but in new circumstances and with new actors.[18]

The dual processes of the disintegration of an existing civilization and the emergence of a new one, described by Toynbee and more specifically outlined by Shoghi Effendi, have been in operation for some time but have become more evident in recent decades, especially since World War I. Among some of the most notable examples of this process of disintegration during the late nineteenth and early twentieth centuries are the dramatic downfall of Napoléon III, the "self-imposed imprisonment of Pope Pius IX in the Vatican," the collapse of the Romanov, the Hohenzollern, and Hapsburg dynasties, "the demise of the Qajar dynasty in Persia," and "the stupendous collapse of both the Sultanate and the Caliphate."[19] These latter two examples refer to the disintegration of the Ottoman Empire, an event of great political and religious significance to Sunni Islam.

In our world, the inevitable process of change is continually weakening the foundations of the older, established institutions and forcing us to reevaluate our long-held and cherished ideas concerning practically every aspect of our lives and beliefs. The alarming level of anxiety and stress experienced by the individual, the bewildering rate of disintegration of the institutions of marriage and the family, the appalling conditions of our educational systems, the confusion surrounding the global economic disorder, the ineffectiveness of old religious belief systems and new ideological doctrines to respond adequately to the needs of contemporary humanity, and the disturbing inability of the political and scientific leaders to find solutions to the problems facing mankind are some examples of the disintegration of our current civilization.

We are now poised at the brink of a change, universal in its magnitude, which will require a total redirection—even reversal—of our concepts about ourselves and our world. Such a drastic and all-encompassing change will require a willingness to view ourselves and our world from a new perspective and, at the same time, to abandon some of our most dearly-held views about the world and our role in it.

> If long-cherished ideals and time-honored institutions, if certain social assumptions and religious formulae have ceased to promote the welfare of the generality of mankind, if they no longer minister to the needs of a continually evolving humanity, let them be swept away and relegated to the limbo of obsolescent and forgotten doctrines. Why should these, in a world subject to the immutable law of change and decay, be exempt from the deterioration that must needs overtake every human institution? For legal standards, political and economic theories are solely designed to safeguard the interests of humanity as a whole, and not humanity to be crucified for the preservation of the integrity of any particular law or doctrine. [20]

The president of the Club of Rome, in his review of the challenges facing humanity, has made similar remarks: "The real challenge....resides in a renewal, even a reversal, of principles and norms which we considered untouchable because they accompanied us in our ascent when we were not proceeding by leaps and bounds and we were not so powerful as to be the main agents of change on earth."[21]

This new way of looking at the world and the willingness to welcome change, especially if it is to improve the condition of humanity and bring it closer to the goals of universal peace and harmony, is yet another step in humanity's march towards growth and maturity—a maturity which does not end in old age, decay, and death but is, rather, a continuous process of increasing knowledge and deepening love, resulting in an ever-advancing civilization characterized by harmony, beauty, and peace.

The emerging awareness that harmony and peace are natural states of the living world and that disharmony and war are unnatural conditions and signs of serious malfunction and illness is of profound importance. This awareness allows us, for the first time, truly to understand the cause of the illness and to remedy it. Until very recently, it was thought that division, competition, and struggle for dominance were natural qualities. However, as Capra observes: "The more one studies the living world the more one comes to realize that the tendency to associate, establish links, live inside one another and cooperate is an essential characteristic of living organisms."[22] Ervin Laszlo beautifully sums up the progress and evolution of life and mankind when he says, "There is a progression from multiplicity and chaos to oneness and order."[23] It is towards this oneness and order that the people of the world are attracted and are now willing to work.

The emerging awareness concerning peace, therefore, is based on solid ground, scientifically and historically. Both these processes have brought us to our present level of readiness to contribute to the cause of peace. Still, before we proceed, we need to understand the nature of peace and the conditions required to ensure its achievement.

3

On the Nature of Peace and Happiness

We should continually be establishing new bases for human happiness and creating and promoting new instrumentalities toward this end. How excellent, how honorable is man if he arises to fulfil his responsibilities; how wretched and contemptible, if he shuts his eyes to the welfare of society and wastes his precious life in pursuing his own selfish interests and personal advantages. Supreme happiness is man's and he beholds the signs of God in the world and in the human soul, if he urges on the steed of high endeavors in the arena of civilization and justice.
—'Abdu'l-Bahá

Peace and happiness have always been and continue to be two of mankind's most elusive goals. As individuals, we all desire happiness and search for it in many different ways. Likewise, on a collective level, peace remains the most sought-after goal.

Usually, when we seek something with all our hearts and minds and work diligently towards achieving it, we will, after the passage of some time, either accomplish our goal or realize that what we seek is unrealistic. If the latter is the case, we will abandon our pursuit. The dilemma we face in respect to peace, however, is that though we have not achieved peace after considerable time, neither have we reached the conclusion that it is an unrealistic goal to be abandoned. Therefore, we need to reevaluate our understanding of the nature of peace and view the whole phenomenon from a new perspective. Before describing this new approach to the question of peace, it will be of value to review some of the similarities and interconnections between peace and happiness.

Pursuit of Happiness: A Persistent Myth

Human happiness is founded upon spiritual behaviour.
　—'Abdu'l-Bahá

The idea of "the pursuit of happiness" is so deeply rooted in our way of thinking that we have difficulty in accepting any other approach. However, most people who spend much time and energy "pursuing" happiness usually find themselves unhappy and disappointed in the end. In the technologically advanced and economically wealthy regions of the world, people are gradually beginning to realize that happiness is not guaranteed by wealth, health, and security. While the majority of people in these countries enjoy high levels of wealth and comfort, have access to the best health facilities, and live under safe and secure circumstances, it would be folly to consider all or even a substantial number of these people as truly happy. They may be content with their conditions, excited about their life activities, and gratified in respect to their desires, and yet they usually continue to seek happiness. As Gorney observes, ". . .direct 'pursuit of happiness' is bound to lead to disappointment. That is why even those who can afford to devote themselves completely to directly pursuing happiness so often are nevertheless forced to seek psychological treatment."[1]

If we reflect on the situations in which we consider ourselves happy, we can identify four distinct circumstances. The first and most common condition which people consider necessary to bring happiness is the gratification of their basic needs, such as food, shelter, health, sex, and physical comfort. In fact, the majority of the world's people are deprived of one or more of these things and consequently are, to some degree, unhappy. However, it is also a fact that the majority of people in the Western world have most or all of these basic needs satisfied, but many remain quite unhappy. The main reason for this is the fact that human happiness depends on much more than the gratification of physical needs and wants. If human

22

happiness were solely dependent upon physical and sexual gratification, then, as Einstein said, "Happiness is for pigs."[2]

The second condition which brings people happiness occurs when they are respected, accepted, and loved by others. The quest for love is universal, and love's close relationship to happiness is undeniable. In fact, under many circumstances, people are willing to forego their physical needs and pleasures in order to obtain greater levels of care and love; thus, love and unity not only bring happiness, but also facilitate the growth process of all people. As 'Abdu'l-Bahá states, ". . .happiness of mankind lieth in the unity and the harmony of the human race, and. . .the spiritual and material developments are conditional upon love and amity among all men."[3]

The third common cause of happiness is human accomplishment. Whenever we accomplish a task, discover a new fact, build a new instrument, or overcome a handicap, we become full of joy and happiness. Even when we read stories of people's lives or watch such movies, we share in the joy of their accomplishment and the sorrow of their failure.

This condition can be explained by the fact that happiness is a state of being in which at least two conditions exist. The first is the existence of a harmony of thought, feeling, and action, while the second is the dedication of these thoughts, feelings, and actions to the development of our true selves as spiritual and noble beings. Happiness, therefore, is felt whenever one's thoughts, feelings, and actions are both united and exalted, creating conditions of inner harmony and ongoing healthy growth.

Human thoughts, feelings, and actions are related to the spiritual capacities of knowledge, love, and will. Through the coordinated and harmonious relationship of knowledge, love, and will, our scientific discoveries, artistic accomplishments, and interpersonal relationships are achieved. It is clear that without these qualities and, consequently, these achievements, our humanness would be endangered and our capacity and opportunities for happiness would decrease dramatically.

Human happiness depends on the affirmation of our true reality, which transcends physical and material well-being and requires a profound understanding of our spiritual nature. 'Abdu'l-Bahá refers to the development of this nature as a prerequisite for happiness when he writes: ". . .the happiness and greatness, the rank and station, the pleasure and peace, of an individual have never consisted in his personal wealth, but rather in his excellent character, his high resolve, the breadth of his learning, and his ability to solve difficult problems."[4] In this passage, 'Abdu'l-Bahá refers to the spiritual qualities of knowledge, love, and will, and identifies their harmonious growth as a prerequisite for individual happiness.

Bahá'u'lláh identifies happiness in the following manner: "In this station," the individual ". . .pierceth the veils of plurality, fleeth from the worlds of the flesh, and ascendeth into the heaven of singleness. . . .He looketh on all things with the eye of oneness, and seeth the brilliant rays of the divine sun shining from the dawning-point of Essence alike on all created things, and the lights of singleness reflected over all creation."[5]

A closer look at these various kinds of happiness will show that there are, in fact, different developmental stages and types, beginning with the most elementary and concrete form, physical gratification, and ending with the most complete and abstract, reflected in the experience of oneness with God. Furthermore, these hierarchical stages and types of happiness all have one fundamental common denominator, which is unity.

At the level of physical happiness and gratification, unity is manifested in the form of health, the result of the harmonious functioning of the different parts of the body by virtue of proper nutrition and care. Furthermore, happiness emanating from love in interpersonal relationships is clearly the by-product of the existence of a state of unity between ourselves and others. In fact, the greater the measure of our interpersonal unity, the greater the level of our love and, consequently, our happiness.

Likewise, happiness, which is the result of human accomplishment in the arenas of science, art, technology, or self-development, is also a reflection of a condition of unity, this time among the inner capacities of knowledge, love, and will. Any successful human endeavour is the result of putting all that one knows into action, to the best of one's ability with the full depth of dedication and love. If we reflect on our lives, we see that the times when we feel happiest are those when our actions are in harmony with our desires and knowledge. Consequently, it is the unity of the inner capacities of knowledge, love, and will which brings us high levels of joy and happiness.

Finally, the highest form of happiness comes from attaining a condition of unity with our main object of love, our Creator. This unity is the ultimate step in our journey towards wholeness. It allows us to delay gratification, to prefer others over ourselves, to live a life of inner oneness and peace, and finally, by connecting ourselves with the Creator, to become creative individuals, promoting a creativity which engenders life and growth and love.

It is clear that the prerequisite for happiness is a condition of unity—within oneself, between self and others, and between self and Creator. And so, it is true that, as George Bernard Shaw said, "Happiness and beauty are by-products. Folly is the direct pursuit of happiness and beauty."[6]

Unity: The Prerequisite for Peace

The doors of love and unity have been unlocked.
　—Bahá'u'lláh

If, in spite of all the efforts of humanity, peace has remained an elusive goal, this is so because the achievement of peace, like that of happiness, is conditional on the existence of certain prerequisites. When these are met, a state of mental and physical tranquillity, as well as freedom from strife and war, is attained. Just as the main prerequisite for achieving happiness is the attainment of unity, similar prerequisites hold true for the establishment of peace. Therefore, we must investigate which conditions must be created in our individual and collective lives to hasten the emergence and strengthen the foundations of a universal peace.

Earlier, the disease of disunity was identified as fertile ground for the development of war. One may conclude that the main prerequisite of peace is the establishment of those conditions which allow people to like and trust one another, and thereby to benefit from one another's experience and knowledge. On the surface, it seems that this is a logical and practical solution to the problem of war. However, these solutions to the issues of war and peace ask us to accept, like, trust, and interact with all people without exception, and such a demand, one may argue, is far too unrealistic. After all, one may ask, what about those people who are evil and criminal, or those who are misguided, unreliable, and untrustworthy? What about those who are careless, lazy, and selfish? The primitive, barbaric, and violent? Those who are ugly, offensive, and have communicable diseases? What about those who are strange, crazy, and unreasonable? Heathens, idol worshippers, and ungodly—or those who are stupid, passive, and unmotivated? What about those who are boring, uncreative, and unpleasant? What about those who are yellow, black, or white? And the list goes on.

We are willing to accept all people as equal, noble, and likeable as ourselves, as long as we are not required to deal with them directly. This is the major stumbling block in the quest to achieve peace. The reason for our inability to accept all people unconditionally is not because we are insincere in our desire for peace, but because we have not fully comprehended the reasons necessitating such a drastic change in our interpersonal and international modes of behaviour.

An unconditional acceptance of all people and nations of the world depends on our capacity to understand the concept of the unity of mankind. Acceptance of this concept depends on our evolution beyond the present level of collective adolescence and our arrival at mankind's age of maturity. In turn, our ability to move beyond the adolescent age depends on willingness to change our views, to modify our behaviour, and to alter our objectives in such a manner that we are able to accept all people unconditionally. Therefore, to achieve unity, we need to live a life of unity, a lifestyle hereto unknown to the generality of mankind.

Over a century ago, Bahá'u'lláh stated that "the well-being of mankind, its peace and security are unattainable unless and until its unity is firmly established."[7] This call has its counterpart at the individual level: there, we are challenged, not only with attaining a state of inner unity necessary for creating a full and integrated personal life, but also with achieving an interpersonal unity among individuals and the members of their families, societies, countries, and the world.

To achieve this high level of individual and collective unity, we require a new mind-set: new approaches to the use of power and love in human relationships; a new perspective on freedom, justice, and equality; a new understanding of the roles of religion and science in human affairs; and a new approach to the issue of the equality of men and women. The attainment of world peace, as Bahá'u'lláh attests, is possible only if we are willing to approach this task in a spirit of humility and receptivity:

> O contending peoples and kindreds of the earth! Set your faces towards unity, and let the radiance of its light shine upon you. Gather ye together, and for the sake of God resolve to root out whatever is the source of contention amongst you. Then will the effulgence of the world's great Luminary envelop the whole earth, and its inhabitants become the citizens of one city, and the occupants of one and the same throne.[8]

A positive response to this call requires humility because one of the greatest causes of continuing warfare is pride, which not infrequently motivates generations of people to seek "vengeance" and restore

26

"honour" to their particular group. Likewise, there is a need for receptivity so that people of the world can see the many shared characteristics, aspirations, and qualities which unite them and which constitute the common foundations of humanity.

Part Two:
The Unity
Paradigm

4

Developing a New Mind-Set

*At present universal peace is a matter of great importance, but unity of
conscience is essential, so that the foundation of this matter may
become secure, its establishment firm and its edifice strong.*
   —'Abdu'l-Bahá

*The unleashed might of the atom has changed everything, except our
thinking. We are consequently moving toward an unparalleled
catastrophe. We shall need a substantially new way of thinking if
mankind is to survive.*
   —Albert Einstein

*. . .global confidence in the United Nations may be eroding
dangerously, principally because the fine words spoken from countless
U.N. podiums have too seldom been translated into concrete
expressions of the unity of purpose we often profess.*
   —Pierre Elliott Trudeau

The concept of unity is both simple and complex—simple because everyone has some notion of its nature, and complex because it demands a total
reorientation of views concerning practically every aspect of life. This
section examines some of the most important concepts of the unity paradigm: the concept of oneness, the collective growth of mankind, and the
equality of men and women.

31

The Concept of Oneness

The devils enter uninvited when the house stands empty.
For other kinds of guests, you have first to open the door.
  —Dag Hammarskjøld

While scientific and technological developments have made the world small by bringing diverse peoples together, obliterating barriers of distance and time through modern means of communication, and creating a world-wide condition of economic, ecological, and political interdependence, people insist on accentuating their differences and focussing on the superficial factors which divide rather than unite them. Thus, the challenge before us today is that of achieving oneness.

The concept of oneness recognizes that the true natures of the most important realities known to mankind are based on the principle of oneness, and includes the reality of the oneness of mankind, of religion, and of God. The concept of the oneness of mankind calls for a fundamental change in our view of relationships among people. From this perspective, neither the cancer of individualism nor the lost identity of collectivism is acceptable. Rather, humanity is viewed as one organic body composed of individuals who, according to their unique characteristics and qualities, form the diversified yet harmonious cells and organs. Thus, the body of mankind functions through the unified, specialized functions of all its constituent parts. Every human being is a part of this organic entity, and his health or illness, his exaltation or debasement, his joy or sorrow, ultimately affects the whole organism. The awareness of this essential oneness is now apparent in all fields of human endeavour. For example, one of the more advanced views of life on this planet comes from Systems Theory:

> The systems view looks at the world in terms of relationships and integration. Systems are integrated wholes whose properties cannot be reduced to those of smaller units. Instead of concentrating on basic building blocks or basic substances, the systems approach emphasizes basic principles of organization.[1]

In recent years, the proponents of Systems Theory have developed a new way of looking at the physical, biological, psychological, social, and cultural aspects of life, and have demonstrated the need for a change in our perspective of the world: "The universe is no longer seen as a machine, made up of a multitude of separate objects, but appears as a harmonious indivisible whole; a network of dynamic relationships that include the human observer and his or her consciousness in an essential way."[2]

A similar perspective of humanity has emerged in the most unexpected area of human sciences—human evolution. This theory, which was first effectively expressed by Darwin, soon became the main scientific framework within which the origins of man and his evolution have been studied during the last century. The predominant and most widely popularized views put forward by these scientists have been that man is, by nature, an aggressive and competitive animal who is, to a large extent, controlled by his instinctual and animalistic drives toward division and separation. However, the most recent findings of scientists in this field point to the opposite conclusion. Leakey and Lewin make the following statements in the concluding section of their book, *Origins*:

> The future of human species depends crucially on two things: our relationships with one another, and our relationship to the world around us. The study of human origins can offer important emphasis in the way we view these two issues.
>
> First, we are one species, one people. Every individual on this earth is a member of *Homo sapiens sapiens*, and the geographical variations we see among peoples are simply biological nuances on the basic theme. The human capacity for culture permits its elaboration in widely different and colorful ways. The often very deep differences between those cultures should not be seen as divisions between people. Instead, cultures should be interpreted for what they really are: the ultimate declaration of belonging to the human species.[3]

The same clear and unequivocal realization of the oneness of humanity is evident in the words and deeds of many thoughtful and concerned scientists, statesmen, and leaders of the contemporary world. The late Aurelio Peccei, former president of the Club of Rome, and Alexander King, its current president, drew a comparison between the health of an organism and the health of the world of humanity, making the following observation:

> The simplest truths are the surest ones. That the health of the parts of any organism, for instance the human body, contributes to the soundness of the whole, and that the state of this whole conditions the functioning of each part, is an accepted truth. We

easily recognize such a truth, but are reluctant to apply it to the world system. And yet modern society is caught in a race in which its own survival is at stake. . . .[4]

Over a century ago, Bahá'u'lláh, in his address to the political leaders of the world, drew an analogy between the world of humanity and the human body, commented on the state of health and illness of this body, made a diagnosis of the causes of its illness, and offered treatment. That same diagnosis and treatment is now, after a lapse of more than a century, finally being discovered by the contemporary scientific, academic, and political leadership of the world. Bahá'u'lláh wrote:

> O ye the elected representatives of the people in every land! Take ye counsel together, and let your concern be only for that which profiteth mankind, and bettereth the condition there-of. . . .Regard the world as the human body which, though at its creation whole and perfect, hath been afflicted, through various causes, with grave disorders and maladies. . . .We behold it, in this day, at the mercy of rulers so drunk with pride that they cannot discern clearly their own best advantage. . . .And when-ever any one of them hath striven to improve its condition, his motive hath been his own gain, whether confessedly so or not; and the unworthiness of this motive hath limited his power to heal or cure.

> That which the Lord hath ordained as the sovereign remedy and mightiest instrument for the healing of all the world is the union of all its peoples in one universal Cause. . . .[5]

The second reality relating to the concept of oneness also calls for a change in our mind-set and is related to conscience, thoughts, and ideas. It is a popular belief that the ideologies emanating from different religious, political, and philosophical sources are irreconcilable. However, in the same manner that all scientific truths are one, all spiritual truths are also one, and the diversity of ideologies is due to the limitations of understand-ing and the differences of perspective.

The Bahá'í view of religion is interesting and novel. It states that all religions are one in their essence, and their apparent differences are due to the varying degrees of capacities and limitations of people and the progres-sive nature of religious revelation. The Bahá'í teachings point out that in the same manner that humanity during its long march towards maturity has learned more about the physical world (science), it has also become capable of much greater insight into spiritual realities (religion). Religions are all expressions of the same spiritual reality, and their progressive revelation is the proof of their oneness. The fact that humanity has perverted the nature of religion and has allowed it to be the cause of separation rather than of the oneness of people is no different from humanity's use of science for the purpose of destruction and warfare rather than for construction and peace. The second aspect of the concept of oneness, therefore, not only refers to the oneness of all religions, but also to the oneness of religion and science, which will be discussed more fully later. The essential issue here is that the oneness of religion is not only a reality but also a necessity in the over-all movement of humanity towards peace. Since religion is the main source of enrichment for the conscience and the enlightenment of the human mind, the unity of religion results in unity of conscience, an essential prerequisite for peace. 'Abdu'l-Bahá states, ". . . until the minds of men become united, no important matter can be accomplished," and further, that ". . . universal peace is a matter of great importance, but unity of conscience is essential, so that the foundation of this matter may become secure, its establishment firm and its edifice strong."[6] In a similar vein, the constitution of UNESCO asserts, "Since war begins in the mind of man, it is in the minds of men that the defence of peace must be constructed. . . ."

The third reality which demands a fundamental change in our mind-set is the concept of the oneness of God. Every human being believes in a god, a god of science or religion, of nationalism or tribalism, of capitalism or socialism, of peace or war, of gratification or self-denial. These and many other gods rule people's lives, give meaning to their activities, provide purpose for their existence, and shape the qualities and the character of their lives. For attainment of humanity's oneness, however, these gods have to be discarded and in their place must come the understanding and realization that the oneness of God, the God of mercy, of love, of enlightenment, and of creativity, is at the very core of all other onenesses and is the object of every human being's deepest yearning.

The importance of this issue becomes clearer when we consider the malignant and destructive consequences of choosing any other god. In his book, *The Promised Day is Come*, Shoghi Effendi refers very movingly to the consequences of such a process. Commenting on the loss of influence of true religion in modern life, he writes:

This vital force is dying out, this mighty agency has been scorned, this radiant light is obscured, this impregnable stronghold abandoned, this beauteous robe discarded. God Himself has indeed been dethroned from the hearts of men, and an idolatrous world passionately and clamorously hails and worships the false gods which its own idle fancies have fatuously created, and its misguided hands so impiously exalted. The chief idols in the desecrated temple of mankind are none other than the triple gods of Nationalism, Racialism and Communism, at whose altars governments and peoples, whether democratic or totalitarian, at peace or at war, of the East or of the West, Christian or Islamic, are, in various forms and different degrees, now worshipping. Their high priests are the politicians and the worldly-wise, the so-called sages of the age; their sacrifice, the flesh and blood of the slaughtered multitudes; their incantations outworn shibboleths and insidious and irreverent formulas; their incense, the smoke of anguish that ascends from the lacerated hearts of the bereaved, the maimed, and the homeless.

The theories and policies, so unsound, so pernicious, which deify the State and exalt the nation above mankind, which seek to subordinate the sister races of the world to one single race, which discriminate between the black and the white, and which tolerate the dominance of one privileged class over all others—these are the dark, the false, and the crooked doctrines for which any man or people who believe in them, or acts upon them, must, sooner or later, incur the wrath and chastisement of God.[7]

The three onenesses—of God, religion, and humanity—are essential aspects of the paradigm of unity, and their recognition is the hallmark of human maturity. At the lower levels of maturity, man, in his search for a sense of identity and in his quest for establishing his uniqueness, tends to accentuate the differences among people and ascribe less importance to the similarities. However, once man moves beyond the search for identity and quest for supremacy which are characteristics of the childhood and adolescent stages of growth, the seemingly irreconcilable qualities of uniqueness and sameness merge and give way to the concept of oneness, which manifests itself variably in various stages of growth and development.

The Concept of the Collective Growth of Mankind

We in the twentieth century, are concluding an era of
mankind five thousand years in length. . . .We are not in
the situation of Rome at the beginning of the Christian
West, but in that of the year 3000 B.C. We open our eyes
like prehistoric man, we see a world totally new.
  —Kurt W. Marek [C. W. Ceram]

Violence is here,
In the words of the sane,
And violence is a symptom.
I hear it in the headlong weeping of men who have failed.
I see it in the terrible dreams of boys
Whose adolescence repeats all history.
  —Jacob Bronowski

One of the most challenging concepts put forward by Bahá'u'lláh is the concept of the collective growth of humanity, which Shoghi Effendi describes in the following manner:

> The long ages of infancy and childhood, through which the human race had to pass, have receded into the background. Humanity is now experiencing the commotions invariably associated with the most turbulent stage of its evolution, the stage of adolescence, when the impetuosity of youth and its vehemence reach their climax, and must gradually be superseded by the calmness, the wisdom, and the maturity that characterize the stage of manhood. Then will the human race reach that stature of ripeness which will enable it to acquire all the powers and capacities upon which its ultimate development must depend.[8]

Adolescence is a period of change, chaos, and confusion. It is a time when human passions are strong—emotions which have caused the destruction, disharmony, and disorder rampant in today's world. However, as humanity grows from its adolescent stage into a stage of maturity, a new set of circumstances, essential for unity and peace, comes into being. It is towards the achievement of maturity and, therefore, oneness of mankind that we must dedicate our efforts and abilities.

The concept of the unity of mankind, as Shoghi Effendi points out:

. . .implies an organic change in the structure of present-day society, a change such as the world has not yet experienced . . . .It calls for no less than the reconstruction and the demilitarization of the whole civilized world—a world organically unified in all the essential aspects of its life, its political machinery, its spiritual aspiration, its trade and finance, its script and language, and yet infinite in the diversity of the national characteristics of its federated units.[9]

The reconstruction and demilitarization of the world is possible for the first time in history, as humanity is at last approaching its age of maturity. During the childhood and adolescent periods in the life of the world's nations, rivalries and competition abound, mainly because of the profound sense of doubt and fear present during these stages. In our world today, it is difficult to identify one nation or government that has reached a level of maturity enabling it to approach others with courage, love, assurance, and true respect. In fact, the more powerful a nation is, the more suspicious, fearful, arrogant, and disrespectful it seems to be.

In current world affairs, the prevalence of rivalry, competition, distrust, suspicion, and arrogance, all characteristics of formative stages of growth, similarly indicates that humanity is at its adolescent stage of growth. The adolescent period, as every student of human behaviour recognizes, is also a period of intense preoccupation with power, pleasure, and love—forces which have great importance in shaping the world today. Also of issue in our world is the relationship between violence and war on the one hand, and the striving for power on the other.

Striving for power is often related to fear, with the accompanying need to conceal one's fear from others and, most important, from oneself. However, because power in itself creates more fear, the process evolves into a cycle where one seeks power to feel more secure but, instead, becomes more insecure as a result of the suspicion and envy of others. Eventually, the frustrated and fearful individuals engaged in this process resort to violence in the hope of eliminating the other party or parties involved in the power struggle.

The periods immediately before the First and Second World Wars are excellent examples of a cycle of mutual fear, mistrust, and suspicion among nations, resulting in a phenomenal increase in armies and armaments, and ultimately leading to the eruption of world-engulfing conflicts. However, the behaviour of the nations and governments after the end of each of these wars was equally destructive and immature. As soon as the period of active hostilities receded, they once again created a scenario of in-groups and out-groups, of "good guys" and "bad guys," "friends" and "enemies," with different members participating in each adolescent camp, making the world an arena for their juvenile war games.

The adolescent mentality of humanity during the twentieth century has been so dominant that we have collectively adopted it, consequently viewing both our lives and our world from an unhealthy adolescent perspective. Our music, clothes, food, hobbies, work habits, sexual orientation, personal ambitions, and value systems are, to a very large degree, those of an adolescent, and we are so immersed in this mentality that we have lost our objectivity.

One of the most important and potentially dangerous characteristics of the adolescent period is unwillingness to heed advice and accept guidance. An adolescent tends to feel that his identity and selfhood will be threatened if he listens to the advice of others or considers their opinions. This quality has frequently led mankind to take lightly the warnings of insightful and concerned individuals who are able to see the dangers engulfing the world and who make heroic attempts to warn adolescent humanity about the destructive consequences of such an attitude.

Over a century ago, Bahá'u'lláh, commenting on the afflictions of humanity and the prevalence of arrogance and conceit in the leaders of the adolescent world, made the following statement:

> We can well perceive how the whole human race is encompassed with great, with incalculable afflictions. We see it languishing on its bed of sickness, sore-tried and disillusioned. They that are intoxicated by self-conceit have interposed themselves between it and the Divine and infallible Physician. Witness how they have entangled all men, themselves included, in the mesh of their devices. They can neither discover the cause of the disease, nor have they any knowledge of the remedy. They have conceived the straight to be crooked, and have imagined their friend an enemy.[10]

A few decades later, during his journey to the West, 'Abdu'l-Bahá warned humanity of an impending world war. The *Montreal Daily Star*, in its issue of September 11, 1912, carried an editorial about 'Abdu'l-Bahá's views on the need for universal peace and the imminence of a world war in Europe. In part, the editorial reads:

'Abdu'l-Bahá has preached Universal Peace for fifty years. . . .In a word, 'Abdu'l-Bahá is the great protagonist of peace in the world today. . . . 'Abdu'l-Bahá, with all his hatred of war and horror at its moral and material results, has no delusions as to the conditions in Europe today or the trend of political events. 'It is futile to hope for a slackening of the present race of the nations to increase their armaments,' he says. 'A great war in Europe is a certainty before permanent peace can be established. International peace can only be reached by an international agreement entered into by all nations. . . .'

Further to this reference concerning the prediction of war, in his biography of 'Abdu'l-Bahá, the Bahá'í historian H. M. Balyuzi writes:

'Abdu'l-Bahá said many a time during His tour of Europe and America, that Europe was like an arsenal, and it needed just one spark to set it ablaze. And it happened as He had foreseen. Subsequent to that carnage of the First World War, sadly viewing the plight of mankind, He stated categorically that 'another war, fiercer than the last, will assuredly break out.'[11]

Several decades later in 1938, Shoghi Effendi made similar observations and gave equally emphatic warnings about the impending outbreak of the Second World War. He wrote:

The earth is now transformed into an armed camp. As much as fifty million men are either under arms or in reserve. No less than the sum of three billion pounds is being spent, in one year, on its armaments. The light of religion is dimmed and moral authority disintegrating. The nations of the world have, for the most part, fallen a prey to battling ideologies that threaten to disrupt the very foundations of their dearly-won political unity. Agitated multitudes in these countries see them with discontent, are armed to the teeth, are stampeded with fear, and groan beneath the yoke of tribulations engendered by political strife. . . .[12]

Shoghi Effendi's warning and predictions were soon realized when destructive forces, motivated by doctrines of national and racial supremacy, characteristics of a competitive and arrogant adolescent world, ignited the fire of the Second World War. However, mankind's reaction to the consequences of this war was also lamentably inadequate, and consequently we again face a similar situation.

That we must grow out of the adolescent phase of our collective growth is unavoidable; the question is how we will achieve this objective, which, in turn, depends upon our collective response to the needs of humanity at this phase of its growth. We must approach our present-day crisis with a totally new orientation and with far more courage than we have done in the past. The Universal House of Justice, the international governing body of the Bahá'í world community, in its November 16, 1969, message to the Bahá'ís of the world, called upon Bahá'ís to dedicate themselves "to consciously strive to be more loving, more united, more dedicated and prayerful than ever before in order to overcome the atmosphere of present-day society which is unloving, disunited, careless of right and wrong and heedless of God." In the same message, the Universal House of Justice commented on "the worsening world situation, fraught with pain of war, violence and the sudden uprooting of long-established institutions," clear indications (as observed repeatedly by Bahá'u'lláh, 'Abdu'l-Bahá, and Shoghi Effendi) of the inability of a "lamentably defective social system, an unenlightened leadership and a rebellious and unbelieving humanity"[13] to solve its current problems.

In the words of the Universal House of Justice:

> Governments and peoples of both the developed and developing nations, and other human institutions, secular and religious, finding themselves helpless to reverse the trend of the catastrophic events of the day, stand bewildered and overpowered by the magnitude and complexity of the problems facing them. At this fateful hour in human history many, unfortunately, seem content to stand aside and wring their hands in despair or else join in the babel of shouting and protestation which loudly objects, but offers no solution to the woes and afflictions plaguing our age.[14]

The reality of humanity's collective growth is one of the most positive aspects of our world today. Although we are still entangled in the mesh of our adolescent drives, perspectives, and intrigues, we are nevertheless becoming aware of the relationship between our collective growth and world challenges and difficulties. The transition from adolescence to maturity, inconceivable at the beginning of the adolescent phase, becomes irresistible in the end, and the individual, impelled by the force of growth and vision of maturity, begins to use his will to hasten this process. The same dynamics are now operative in humanity's collective life. Having become aware of the dangers of undue continuation of our adolescence and imminent fulfillment of our historical longing for unity and peace, more and more of us find ourselves immensely drawn to life in a mature and united world. One indication of this quest for maturity is the ever-expanding number of individuals around the world who are dedicating themselves to the creation of the specific prerequisites for a mature human society, such as the equality of men and women, eradication of all forms of prejudice, and creation of a more equitable socioeconomic system, to give only a few of the most obvious examples.

The Reality of the Equality of Men and Women

Do you want to enjoy her love, or do you want to dominate it?
—John Drinkwater

Attempts at developing a "unity mind-set" will be unsuccessful until the reality of the equality between the sexes is adequately understood, its importance fully acknowledged, and its implementation unhesitatingly pursued. It is folly to expect unity and peace in the family of mankind until the two halves of the world population, women and men, are truly equal and have the same degree of influence in world affairs. 'Abdu'l-Bahá asserts, "Without equality this [peace] will be impossible because all differences and distinction are conducive to discord and strife."[15] He also says, "When all mankind shall receive the same opportunity of education and the equality of men and women be realized, the foundations of war will be utterly destroyed."[16]

In order to appreciate various aspects of the relationship between the issues of sexual equality and unity, we need to define equality, to understand the dynamics of interpersonal relationships in a truly equal situation, and to contemplate the roles of men and women in waging war and creating peace.

While various definitions of the word "equal" exist, the one most applicable to this issue follows: ". . .having the same rights, privileges and rank" in such a manner that the situation is "fair, just and impartial."[17] Fairness, justice, and impartiality are archaic definitions of the word "equal," yet they have as much relevance today as they did in the past. A study of history shows that women in all societies have never had the same rights, privileges, and rank as men, nor have they ever been recipients of fair, just, and impartial treatment. Some of the more obvious reasons for this inequity relate to power and pleasure in human relationships. Just as in the world of childhood and adolescence where physical power rules supreme, in the evolving communities of humanity men have held on to their power both at home and in the community. Likewise, pleasure and gratification play very important roles during childhood and adolescence. Consequently men, by virtue of their superior physical powers, have always used, and continue to use, women as objects of pleasure and gratification.

The human mind, however, has the capacity to perceive power and pleasure in a seemingly contradictory manner. In other words, we frequently encounter a power relationship in which both the dominant and the dominated derive gratification and pleasure and so encourage the maintenance of the unequal status quo which exists between them. Although these power dynamics are basically of a psychosocial nature, their remedies are not necessarily found in psychological analyses and therapies, or in sociological reforms and reorientation. Though these methods are necessary, they are not sufficient to bring about true equality between men and women. Rather, the solution lies in our understanding the true nature of human reality.

When we speak of equality, we must bear in mind the observable fact that some people are better endowed than others in respect to physical strength, intellectual capacities, or artistic talents. Furthermore, not all people have the same opportunity for a good education and upbringing. Therefore, to make a statement that all people have the same rights, privileges, and rank is more of an expression of hope than a reality which can truly be accomplished.

The equality of rights, privileges, and rank is possible, however, if we acknowledge the spiritual nature of human reality. If human nature is perceived mainly as physical nature, then there is no doubt that people in general, and women and men in particular, are not created equal. The

43

concept of humanity's spiritual nature introduces a new dimension into the question of equality—the dimension of humanness.

All people possess the human capacities to be aware, knowledgeable, and insightful; to give and receive love and compassion; to care; to decide; and to act in a purposeful, meaningful manner. What differentiates people is their mode of expressing these spiritual qualities. Thus, all people love, but each in his or her unique manner; all people possess insights and understanding unique to each individual and make decisions according to personal circumstances and objectives. It is in respect to both the universality of spiritual qualities and the uniqueness of individual characteristics that people are equal, and so men and women must be treated equally in respect to their rights and privileges as unique and spiritually-endowed individuals. Society must provide them with opportunities to evolve and grow to the fullness of their potential. In this way, every human being, every woman and man, will eventually reflect the wisdom, the beauty, and the creativity of her or his Creator. Once this happens, the issues of rank, fairness, and justice are resolved. In the same manner that, in a flower garden, every flower has its own beauty, colour, and fragrance, in the garden of humanity there are varieties of people who, by their very existence as unique beings, add to the richness and the beauty of the world.

Having reviewed the issue of equality in general, we are now in a position to focus on the dynamics of the man-woman relationship in a condition of true equality. From the outset, it is clear that two individuals can relate to one another as equals if they have developed an understanding of the nature of equality. In other words, a woman and a man, both of whom are mature and united in their understanding of the need for equality, will have a better chance of establishing an equal relationship than will individuals without these qualities.

An equal relationship calls for cooperation rather than competition, flexibility rather than rigidity, others-directedness rather than self-centredness, tenderness rather than forcefulness, and humility rather than arrogance. These are characteristics of maturity which demonstrate that the true equality of men and women is conditional upon humanity's growth to its collective level of maturity. Conversely, humanity as a whole cannot achieve maturity until it focusses attention and efforts on achieving the equality of women and men. 'Abdu'l-Bahá likens the world of humanity to a bird, with men and women as its two wings. This bird will not make its flight to the heights of glory until the two wings are equal: "Should one wing remain weak, flight is impossible."[18] "As long as women are prevented from attaining their highest possibilities," 'Abdu'l-Bahá also asserts, ". . .so long will men be unable to achieve the greatness which might be theirs."[19] He further states, "The happiness of mankind will be realized when women and men coordinate and advance equally. . . ."[20]

Another fact significant to the issue of equality is complementarity. At present, women, in their attempts to achieve equality, stress that, in and by themselves, they are as capable as men in contributing to the welfare of society. This is true, and the comparison is apt. However, surely both women and men are more capable and insightful in all aspects of their lives if they receive the cooperation, assistance, guidance, and participation of the opposite sex in their endeavours.

The need for complementarity in male-female relationships is apparent at all levels: biological, psychological, social, and spiritual. However, nowhere is it more apparent than in respect to the issue of war and peace. War is a game played by juvenile men in order to reassure their fragile egos of their manhood and to impress others with their power. All the major wars of humanity have been fought by men, and even in those instances where women have played a major role, they have merely adopted a leadership style similar to the competitive and power-oriented approach used by men in settling conflicts. However, the impact of large-scale leadership by women in the world will no doubt create dynamics at variance with the power politics of the contemporary world. 'Abdu'l-Bahá provides us with a description of some of the changes that will occur in the world as a result of greater equality between women and men:

> The world in the past has been ruled by force, and man has dominated over woman by reason of his more forceful and aggressive qualities both of body and mind. But the balance is already shifting—force is losing its weight and mental alertness, intuition, and the spiritual qualities of love and service, in which woman is strong, are gaining ascendancy. Hence, the new age will be an age less masculine, and more permeated with the feminine ideals—or, to speak more exactly, will be an age in which the masculine and feminine elements of civilization will be more evenly balanced.[21]

The development of a new mind-set in respect to the equality of men and women, the collective growth of mankind, and the universal concept of oneness will ultimately lead us to the adoption of new types of behaviour and new approaches towards these issues. In any human endeavour, there is first a need for change in perspective and in ideas. Ideas are powerful, and guide the nature of our behaviour and activities, ultimately determining the manner in which we use power and love in human relationships at all levels.

5

Uses and Abuses of Power and Love in Human Relationships

He had not trusted his mother. And he had not trusted that God before whom he had bowed his head to the stone floor for eleven years of his youth. Later he did not trust his own fellow Party members, especially those who spoke well. He did not trust his fellow exiles. He did not trust the peasants to sow grain and reap harvests unless they were coerced and their work was regularly checked on. He did not trust workers to work unless production norms were set for them. He did not trust the members of the intelligentsia not to commit sabotage. He did not trust soldiers and generals to fight without threat of penalty regiments and machine guns in their rear. He did not trust his intimates. He did not trust his wives and mistresses. He did not trust his children. . . .

He had trusted one person, one only, in a life filled with mistrust. Alone among Stalin's enemies, while the whole world watched, he had turned around and offered Stalin his friendship. And Stalin had trusted him. That man was Adolf Hitler.
    —Solzhenitsyn

The narcissist has no interest in the future.
    —Christopher Lasch

47

In the context of human relationships, power and love have always played fundamental roles. However, power is not equally distributed among people. There are those who possess much greater degrees of power by virtue of their social status, economic capacities, educational opportunities, physical strength, or psychological development. This power can be either used, abused, or abdicated, depending on the individual's life circumstances and, more importantly, on his overall understanding of himself and his purpose in life. The same is true for human love, which can be withheld, given with certain conditions attached, or offered in an unconditional and universal manner.

Historically, both power and love have been abused at all levels of human relationships—in the context of marriage, the family, society, and the world at large. The nature of this abuse needs to be understood if we are to develop human relationships where unity reigns, while at the same time retaining the uniqueness of individuals and groups.

In many respects, love and power are interrelated and indivisible. We need certain powers in order to give to other people, to care for them, to encourage them in their activities, to nurture them, and to trust them. The powers most necessary for these accomplishments are those which render us victorious over our selfish desires and self-doubts about our capacity to be generous, encouraging, and trusting. In turn, these powers are developed when we receive love and encouragement from others. Consequently, in healthy relationships, love and power are integrated and reciprocated. However, in most human relationships at the marital, familial, societal, or international level, power has been the dominant force.

The relationship that is based primarily on power has certain characteristics which are identified with authoritarianism by psychologists and social scientists. Although the authoritarian mode of relating has been and remains the most common in human relationships, there are nevertheless two other modes, the indulgent and the integrative, which are worthy of study. While the authoritarian and the indulgent modes display characteristics of childhood and adolescent stages of development, the integrative mode describes a mature type of human relationship, and, therefore, has a special importance in our understanding of the prerequisites for facilitating humanity's transition from its age of adolescence to adulthood.

The Authoritarian Mode

The harvest of force is turmoil and the ruin of social order.
— 'Abdu'l-Bahá

The nature of interpersonal relationships is affected by at least four factors: an understanding of one's purpose in life, one's perspective on human nature, the degree of one's emotional maturity, and the nature of one's interaction with others. It is not an easy task to define a purpose for life, and most people do not spend much time pondering this issue. However, in spite of this, we all do have a purpose for our lives, because without one, we would find it very difficult to live. The fact that many people claim an inability to find or define a purpose for their lives does not prove that they have none.

At the most basic level, people have two purposes: to avoid pain and to experience pleasure. The authoritarian approach is primarily centred on the avoidance of pain and has its roots in the fear of powerlessness, a characteristic of childhood and early adolescent periods of life. During these early years, we are painfully aware of our physical, emotional, and intellectual inadequacies and vulnerabilities, and tend to compare ourselves negatively with adults who are seemingly more powerful in every respect.

One major outcome of these feelings of powerlessness and insecurity is the development of a purpose in life based on the acquisition of power. The child, especially if raised in an authoritarian environment, develops an affinity for power and begins to develop a view of life based on pursuit of power, in the hope that more power will bring more security and will eliminate some of his fears and anxieties. He becomes power-oriented,[1] always trying to be in a position of dominance over others; however, because the individual is not alone in this world, he soon encounters others who are also seeking power. Thus, an atmosphere of competition and power struggle begins to develop. In the words of Erich Fromm:

> For the authoritarian character there exist, so to speak, two sexes: the powerful ones and the powerless ones. His love, admiration and readiness for submission are automatically aroused by power, whether of a person or of an institution. Power fascinates him not for any values for which a specific power may stand, but just because it is power. Just as his "love"

is automatically aroused by power, so powerless people or institutions automatically arouse his contempt.[2]

Earlier, it was pointed out that human power in and by itself is not evil; rather, it is a very important and necessary aspect of life, both in the individual and in the society. Rollo May identifies five kinds of power, three destructive and two constructive. The destructive kinds are exploitative, the "most destructive kind of power"; manipulative, used "over another person"; and competitive, used "against another person." The two constructive kinds of power are nutrient, used "for the other person"; and integrative, used "with the other person."[3] It is, therefore, the abuse of power which characterizes the authoritarian human relationship and is its first major feature.

Individuals may also adopt an authoritarian approach to life because of their understanding of human nature. Individually and collectively, children fear unknown factors, imaginary beings, or powerful and evil persons waiting to attack and undermine their integrity or even their lives. In response to such imaginary and real threats, these children (and primitive societies) develop a dichotomous perception of creation. Thus, everything is good or bad, familiar or strange, and people are seen either as friend or enemy, insider or outsider.

Since an authoritarian mode of relating to the world has its roots in the insecurities and fears of the childhood and adolescent stages of development, it should not come as a surprise that this is the most common approach in human relationships. A majority of parents tend to relate to their children in an authoritarian manner; many women are subject to the authoritarian attitude of men; and institutions and governments are commonly organized according to this principle.

In an authoritarian setting, obedience is of paramount importance. Each individual has his place pegged at a certain level and is expected to behave in a manner "appropriate" to that level. Thus, children, students, women, and those who are poor, powerless, and destitute must obey their superiors. In turn, the authoritarian individual submits willingly to the rule of those more powerful than he, as he seeks their approval and love. This phenomenon is called "authoritarian submission"[4] and is another important characteristic of this mode.

In addition to power-orientation, dichotomous perceptions, and authoritarian submission, the authoritarian mode has another far-reaching characteristic—rigidity in the emotional and intellectual spheres.

Authoritarian individuals, institutions, and governments, because of their fears, suspicions, and insecurities, tend to avoid change. They cling to dogma, tradition, and established policies, and approach life in the same way their parents and grandparents approached it. For them, the status quo is much more reassuring than a situation which is constantly changing, evolving, and growing. Thus, creativity, spontaneity, and open-mindedness are not welcome under authoritarian conditions.

This outline of the major characteristics of the authoritarian mode clearly shows the basis of some major interpersonal and international conflicts. It is obvious that the authoritarian mode of government, for example, is more oriented towards disunity, mistrust, and suspicion than towards unity, trust, and confidence in others. However, it should be noted that the authoritarian mode of relating is not confined to dictatorial and undemocratic governments. Democratic institutions and governments also fall prey to this type of behaviour, but in a less obvious manner. In fact, a cursory look at many societies which consider themselves democratic will show that authoritarianism is prevalent at all levels of their social structure. A truly democratic society can exist only in a mature, united, and spiritually-enlightened world, and not in an adolescent world filled with competition, suspicion, and insecurity.

The Indulgent Mode

Our world echoes with the demand for pleasure. . . .
    —Hans Schaefer

Our Western civilization seems to be turning gradually into
*a happy 'Mahagonny' . . . .**
    —Udo Schaefer

Earlier, it was mentioned that pain-avoidance and pleasure-seeking are two examples of a life purpose which, in the early stages of development, are strong and play a role in a person's mode of looking at the world and relating to life. However, pain-avoidance and pleasure-seeking are not always equally influential in the life of an individual, and one or the other

* In the city of Mahagonny everything is allowed except having no money.

may assume predominance in the individual's approach to life. When pleasure-seeking becomes the primary objective in a person's life, we are dealing with an indulgent personality, and likewise, when a society becomes primarily preoccupied with the gratification of needs and wants, an indulgent society emerges. As the quest for instant gratification and the tendency toward self-indulgence are normally found in children and adolescents, similar characteristics are prevalent in adults and societies which are still functioning with a childhood and adolescent mind-set.

Pleasure-orientation, an important characteristic of the indulgent person and society, usually develops in circumstances where material prosperity precedes emotional maturity, allowing for a lifestyle of self-centredness and self-indulgence. Examples of this type of societal orientation are to be found in the Roman Empire before its fall and in twentieth century Western civilization. One of the main reasons for the development of a pleasure-oriented lifestyle is the absence of a well-formulated purpose and meaning in the lives of people. When a society adopts a materialistic and hedonistic approach to life, it discards its reason for being. As a result, the individuals and institutions in that society soon give up hope for growth and development. In his book, *The Culture of Narcissism*, Christopher Lasch describes this process:

> Having no hope of improving their lives in any of the ways that matter, people have convinced themselves that what matters is psychic self-improvement: getting in touch with their feelings, eating health food, taking lessons in ballet or belly-dancing, immersing themselves in the wisdom of the East, jogging, learning how to "relate," overcoming the "fear of pleasure."[5]

Such an approach to life is, in essence, chaotic. All endeavours are aimed at the avoidance of pain and, more importantly, at achieving gratification and pleasure. There is a general unwillingness and inability to set a purpose in life apart from these goals. Any other objective would require discipline, hard work, postponement of gratification, willingness to suffer and experience pain, the ability to work in harmony and cooperation with others, and to be of service to one's fellow man. Such qualities are needed for the creation of a healthy relationship but are almost nonexistent in the life of an indulgent person.

In addition to the promotion of pleasure-orientation and a chaotic lifestyle, the indulgent mode of human communication creates anarchy and disorder both in the individual and in society. The only source of authority and power that the indulgent person acknowledges is gratification. He seeks a freedom similar to that which animals possess: the freedom to gratify biological and instinctual needs and desires, without according due consideration to the other realities of complex human relationships. These individuals rationalize all of their self-centred activities in the name of individual freedom, the freedom to do whatever one pleases as long as it does not interfere with the rights of others. In reality, however, at one level, all people are interrelated. There is a universal ecology of life which, at the level of human relationships, creates a universal interdependence similar to the organs and parts of a body. Thus, for example, the health or illness of one individual ultimately affects others as well. Consequently, the actions of the indulgent individual do interfere with the rights and lives of others. The indulgent individual ignores this fact and, subsequently, introduces anarchy into interpersonal relationships.

Finally, the intellectual and emotional characteristics of an indulgent individual have serious consequences for both the individual and society at large. The continuous pursuit of pleasure often results in a lifestyle characterized by the quest for instant gratification, which, in turn, requires a willingness to sacrifice fundamental principles of quality, integrity, and beauty. In the indulgent lifestyle, emotions are an end in themselves. The individual seeks joy and happiness but refuses to submit to the self-discipline and control required for creativity and growth, prerequisites for true joy and happiness. The indulgent person avoids the pain and discomfort of growth and thus hampers the progress of his own maturity and development.

Briefly, the main characteristics of the indulgent mode of relating are pleasure-orientation, chaotic lifestyle, anarchy in human relationships, and promiscuity in respect to the intellectual and emotional aspects of life. These characteristics are commonly found in our world today and are usually seen coexisting with the authoritarian mode of relating. In fact, in some societies, such as that of North America, both authoritarian and indulgent modes are found at all levels of the society, in the individual parents, in the family, at the workplace, and in the functioning of the government. Likewise, in those societies which seem totally authoritarian, we find that at the individual and interpersonal level people indulge themselves through heavy use of alcohol, wherever possible through drugs and through an extremely promiscuous lifestyle, all in keeping with the adolescent phase in the collective lives of these societies and with the authoritarian and indulgent modes of living.

The Integrative Mode

There is no fear in love; but perfect love casteth out fear.
—St. John

The foregoing descriptions of the authoritarian and indulgent lifestyles demonstrate that, while they are common in childhood and adolescent stages of the individual and collective life of humanity, they are not appropriate for the creation of a mature society. Our challenge is to develop new approaches to love and power, integrating them into a new lifestyle characterized by love-orientation, unity in diversity, responsibility, and creativity—the integrative mode of relating.

The unity paradigm calls for unity not only between people but also within every person. Interpersonal unity calls for love and responsibility, while intrapersonal unity requires harmony between the forces of love and power as well as an ability to be creative, life-engendering, and constructive. Elsewhere, I have described the main characteristics of the integrative mode,[6] from which I will quote extensively to outline the four characteristics of the integrative mode of relating.

First a healthy, integrated person possesses those qualities which can best be described as love-orientation. Love-orientation refers to the concept that we will be most secure, accepted, and admired when we approach others from the position of respect, acceptance, trust, and service. Such an orientation engenders good will, allows sharing, and creates an atmosphere of mutuality and togetherness. In essence, love-orientation leads people to be of service to one another, and makes estrangement and competition between them unnecessary. Under these circumstances all individuals involved have a much greater opportunity to evolve and grow personally and at the same time to contribute to the growth of their society.

A second characteristic of an integrated personality is related to the person's fundamental view of creation. The authoritarian person perceives dichotomies and antagonism everywhere, while the indulgent person refuses to see the distinctions and individuality so clearly abundant in the world of creation and, consequently, develops a chaotic worldview. A balanced, healthy attitude is one which allows the person to perceive the individual characteristics of all people, to realize that every person is unique, beautiful, and important in his own right, and, yet, to acknowledge that all people are equal in respect to their humanness and so must have equal rights and opportunities. The merging of the seemingly contradictory qualities of the uniqueness, diversity, equality, and oneness of people is one of the hallmarks of a healthy personality. This allows the development of an awareness of the unity in diversity which characterizes healthy human relationships.

Both the indulgent person, because of his promiscuous attitude towards his emotions and thoughts, and the authoritarian, by virtue of his emotional and intellectual rigidity, are unable to reach their creative potential. Creativity calls for the freedom to search and experiment, yet it also calls for discipline and order. All of man's great scientific discoveries and artistic achievements are aimed at a better understanding of the order and meaning of the universe. Creativity, therefore, the third characteristic of an integrated personality, becomes most possible when the person is able to free himself from the rigidity of the authoritarian personality and the promiscuity of the indulgent lifestyle and to combine the seemingly contradictory qualities of discipline and order with freedom of search and expression.

The fourth characteristic of a healthy use of power in human relations is directly related to the daily interaction of people. In authoritarian relationships, the authoritarian person demands obedience and submission from all those who are weaker than he while he, in turn, submits without question to the demands and wishes of those who are more powerful than he. In the indulgent relationship, the person is constantly seeking pleasure and engages only in activities which might enhance his chances of attaining further gratification. The predominant consideration is the attainment of pleasure and the avoidance of pain rather than the nature of the relationship and the identity of the person involved.

Unlike the authoritarian and indulgent forms of interaction, power in a healthy relationship is used in a responsible manner in order to foster cooperation and service. Responsibility and cooperation are hallmarks of the mature use of power and are signs of the growth of the individuals involved. Most of the power of the participants in the authoritarian and indulgent modes of communication is wasted, abused, or misused. However, in a cooperative relationship, the power and energy of the participants accumulates and creates opportunities for creativity and service. The following schema compares the characteristics of various types of personalities in relation to power and love in human relationships.

PERSONALITY TYPE / CHARAC-TERISTICS	Authoritarian Personality	Indulgent Personality	Integrative Personality
Orientation	Power-oriented	Pleasure-oriented	Growth-oriented
Worldview	Dichotomous Perceptions	Indiscriminate Perceptions	Unity in Diversity
Emotional and Intellectual Characteristics	Rigidity	Promiscuity	Creativity
Relationships with Others	Authoritarian Submission	Anarchic Relationships	Responsibility and Cooperation

Schema 1: Characteristics of Authoritarian, Indulgent, and Integrative Personalities.

It is clear from this examination that the advent of mankind's age of maturity must coincide with the predominance of the integrative approach to life and human relationships. This is a condition which would use human power in a useful and constructive manner, allow the life-engendering and growth-inducing properties of a mature and enlightened love to permeate human relationships, and facilitate the process of the integration of human love and power into a condition of creativity, beauty, and unity. Ultimately, the unity of love and power will bring about a most dramatic change in human relationships.

6

The Challenge of Freedom

Five great enemies to peace inhabit with us: viz., avarice, ambition, envy, anger, and pride. If those enemies were to be banished, we should infallibly enjoy perpetual peace.
—Petrarch

Freedom lives on the far side of order.
—Frederick Turner

Freedom is a universal goal which, like peace and happiness, has been pursued and yet not completely achieved. As with the pursuit of peace and happiness, it is clear that the main reasons for the inability of humanity to achieve a free world are its disunity and immaturity. A disunited and immature world is usually divided into warring and competing groups, each seeking more power and more dominance over the others, with the natural outcome being the loss of human freedom and the creation of injustice and inequality.

During its childhood and adolescent stages, humanity has had much difficulty freeing itself from the conditions of self-centredness and self-doubt, fertile conditions for the establishment of selfishness and fear. These attitudes, in turn, cause individuals to manifest anger and hatred towards others, who often become scapegoats and lose their freedom in the process.

To emerge from this condition of bondage, inequality, and violence, we first need to study the meaning and nature of freedom. Then, we must return to the theme of human nature and once again try to define human nature, this time in light of the evolving realities of maturity and unity. As new definitions are formulated, new ideas and concepts about freedom will also come into being.

The Meaning and Nature of Freedom

Man's freedom is a freedom to betray God. God may love us—yes—but our response is voluntary.
    —Dag Hammarskjøld

At first glance, the meaning of freedom seems to be straightforward: A person should have certain rights and liberties, as well as responsibilities. One should be free to choose one's style of living, as long as it does not infringe upon the rights of others, and to communicate thoughts and ideas without being censored or punished. Freedom is also equated with maturity and capacity. After all, every mature and capable individual should be free to choose what to drink and eat, how to dress, with whom and under what conditions to have sexual relationships, and the manner in which to convey private thoughts and ideas. Further, for many the concept of freedom includes the liberty to exercise power. Every human being possesses some kind of power—emotional, intellectual, physical, social, material, or other. Power, however, confers both freedom and limitations on the individual and, because of its seductive nature, often tends to be abused. Consequently, power is, not infrequently, very limiting.

In addition to these types of freedom, there is a curious notion of freedom as licence to do wrong as long as it hurts only the individual and no one else. Thus, it is not uncommon to encounter individuals who do all types of damage to their health, intellectual growth, and emotional and spiritual welfare in the name of individual freedom and liberty.

A closer look at these various concepts of freedom will show that they are simplistic, individualistic, and fundamentally erroneous. Although it is true that every individual must have certain basic rights and responsibilities, it is equally true that every individual is a part of the whole body of humanity and, therefore, his health or illness, action or inaction, progression or regression, success or failure, and joy or sadness affect, in a direct or indirect manner, all others. Consequently, human freedom must be understood within the framework of both the individual and collective vicissitudes of human existence. Within such a broad framework, we can identify the following stages and facets of human freedom: freedom from the limitations of physical needs and environmental threats, freedom from the oppression of other human beings, and freedom from self and egotism. Although people have always sought, to some degree, these various forms of freedom, a study of history and the contemporary world show that, at any given time and under different circumstances, one of these three types of freedom predominates. For example, in our world today millions are still slaves to hunger, disease, and forces of nature such as drought and severe climatic changes. However, at the same time millions are also subject to untold tyranny and aggression inflicted upon them by other human beings. Finally, even in those countries where people are not victims of poverty, disease, and war, they are victims of their own immoderate, anxiety-ridden, aggressive, and competitive lifestyles. Furthermore, it should be pointed out that these various types of freedom are hierarchical in nature, and each of them usually assumes urgency once the more primitive, basic needs and threats are dealt with and freedom from their forces is achieved. Thus, there is a need for freedom from egotism and self-centredness in the more affluent and peaceful parts of the world. It is this egotism and self-centredness which not only deprives people of true freedom, but also makes them deny others their freedom.

The most elementary type of freedom is that from the basic physical needs and dangers of hunger, disease, and natural elements. At this level, man and animals are similarly affected, except that man, by virtue of his intelligence, has the knowledge and expertise necessary for the acquisition of adequate nutritious food, the capacity to prevent and treat diseases, and the technology necessary for building a healthy and comfortable habitat for himself.

The present challenge facing humanity is not a lack of knowledge and expertise, but the absence of freedom of a different kind: from egotism, self-centredness, and mistrust. However, for man to achieve this type of freedom, he first requires knowledge. Ignorance is the most limiting force in human life, rendering the individual impotent, fearful, and super-stitious. It causes him to fear his environment, his fellow human beings, and himself. Ignorance, furthermore, results in spending much energy and time in the performance of the simplest tasks. Ignorance also explains reality within the dark and misleading framework of superstition.

However, although man is born without information and knowledge, he is also born with intelligence, a capacity to discover, to understand, and to create. Consequently, over the course of history, man has continually added to his knowledge and has successfully fought the slavery of ignorance.

Once again, the challenge before man is not so much a lack of knowledge as it is a lack of will and motivation to use knowledge in a universal, equitable, and constructive manner—a situation primarily due to one's slavery to self and ego as well as suspicion and mistrust of one's fellow human beings. In fact, one of the most persistent and obvious obstacles to human freedom has always been and remains man's fellow human beings. Throughout history, people have denied others their most basic rights through the abuse of power and the planning of mischief. At one level, this behaviour has been attributed to the physical needs and economic aspirations of people, while at another level, it has been viewed as an indication of human ignorance and its accompanying feelings of fear, superstition, and incompetence.

However, neither the improvement of the physical and material aspects of life nor an increase in knowledge of the world and its people have reduced man's inhumanity to man. Power continues to be abused by the powerful, and slavery of a most brutal and subtle nature continues to be practiced against women, children, minorities, as well as the poor, the sick, the aged, and all others who are downtrodden and devoid of power.

The persistence of this behaviour, in spite of many efforts on the part of concerned individuals and groups, has had profound effects on the thinking of mankind. Today, in schools, universities, and other institutions of learning, as well as in the general population, there exists a strongly-held view that man is indeed evil in his essence, that at best he is an animal with a sophisticated approach to the task of staying alive or, at worst, a machine devoid of true consciousness and conscience. Holding fast to such views naturally renders man more impotent and deprives him of true liberty.

Man will approach the condition of true liberty when he begins to understand himself truly and to live a life which is in harmony with his true nature. In a sense, every human being needs to repeat in his lifetime what humanity has gone through during its existence. Every individual needs to free himself from his instinctual and physical demands; he needs to understand them, to learn to control them, and to use them in the service of higher levels of freedom. Thus, paradoxically, the control of instinctual and physical demands makes it possible for the person to achieve freedom. Furthermore, the same attitude of control will make it possible to acquire knowledge and to advance further the cause of science and technology.

This knowledge will ultimately lead the person out of the domain of self-centredness and isolation to that of others-directedness and universality. True freedom is achieved when the individual becomes aware of the noble, spiritual nature of man and recognizes the fundamental equality and interdependence of all people. It is through interdependence and unity that people will truly feel secure and trustful, and, thus, truly free—impossible in an atmosphere of mistrust and competition. Likewise, it is impossible to feel free in a community of mankind in which people are perceived as being by nature evil, untrustworthy, and fundamentally selfish.

These are some of the major obstacles in man's quest for freedom and liberty. The task before us is to understand how to overcome these obstacles, to investigate the best way of attaining true liberty, and to examine contemporary events or examples which might shed light on this process.

Human Attempts at Self-Definition

I lie there alone, all is still but the ticking of the clock on the wall, 'who are you, what are you, who are you, what are you?' And I start thinking, 'who am I, what am I?' and spend the whole night thinking about it.
—Agafya Mikhailovna, a servant in Tolstoy's household

The prerequisites for attaining true liberty are more readily identified once the processes of human search for meaning and attempts at self-definition are closely studied. These processes are developmental in nature, beginning with simplistic, self-oriented, and grandiose ideas about self and life. In the same manner that the human child sees the world and its people existing simply to satisfy his needs and wants, with everything revolving around him, humanity, collectively, in its era of childhood, also perceived itself to be the most important of all that was created and viewed its habitat, the earth, as the centre of the universe. However, these views were soon to be shattered as, with the advancement of scientific inquiry and methods, new facts about the universe became known.

The Copernican revolution dealt the first great blow to man's view of himself. This scientific revolution showed that man's prized habitat, the earth, was not, after all, the centre of the universe, and man, dethroned from this position of centrality, had to comfort himself with the fact that he was the most noble and unique of all creation. However, according to Freud, a second blow to man's identity came with the Darwinian revolution, which advanced the view of common ancestry for man and animals. The third blow was dealt by Freud himself, who showed that often at the root of human motives are unconscious processes and instinctual drives which operate independently from human will and decision-making faculties.[1]

Bruno Bettelheim, a prominent psychiatrist and survivor of Nazi concentration camps, identifies three other basic blows to man's view of himself. The first occurred as a result of World War I, ". . .which destroyed the belief that in and of itself [scientific] progress would solve our problems, provide meaning to our life, and help us master our existential anxiety—the human fear of death."[2] The second crisis of human identity in this century came as a result of World War II's Auschwitz and Hiroshima, which ". . .showed that progress through technology has escalated man's destructive impulse into more precise and incredibly more devastating form."[3] The third major blow identified by Bettelheim also came as a result of events of World War II and the modern holocausts. These holocausts were not acts of God but, rather, the results of deliberate and calculated decisions by men, which caused suffering and destruction beyond belief. They forced us to realize that both our world picture and our image of man are untrustworthy. Furthermore, they showed that, in spite of all our scientific and technological progress and the good it offers, we are also quite capable of using science as a tool of destruction in well-organized programs of slavery and abuse of others.[4]

These six major crises in the collective identity of mankind have resulted in the development of a view of man as an animal whose activities and behaviour are determined by his instinctual drives and unconscious psychological processes. Furthermore, these views depict man as an intelligent animal who uses his power of intellect to achieve self-gratification, is competitive by nature, and is driven and governed by the laws of the survival of the fittest. In the jungle of civilization that man himself created, laws govern the lives of human beings along the mechanistic demands of technology and the instinctual imperatives of an animalistic nature.

Aside from the view of man determined by these different revolutions, another way which we can understand our attempts to define ourselves is by identifying the major periods in our collective life on earth. Basically, three such phases can be identified, these being the phases of primary union, separation or individuation, and, finally, secondary union.

The phase of primary union in man's growth is, in some ways, parallel to the embryonic period of individual human life. During this phase there is a considerable degree of oneness between mankind and his natural world. In the womb of this world, humanity gradually, over a few million years, grew enough finally to be able to differentiate itself from its natural environment, a phase which Erich Fromm likens to that in which there exist "primary ties" between the embryo and the mother's body, ties which "give him security and a feeling of belonging and of being rooted somewhere."[5]

In an infant, the transition from the stage of primary union to that of individuation and separation takes place soon after birth, occurring when the child separates himself from his mother and begins a social life in which he is an individual, separate from others. During the phase of individuation, the accent is on separation, individuality, comparison, and competition. Though these characteristics are prevalent during the years of childhood and adolescence, they can last throughout the life of the individual, who may never reach the phase of secondary union. Erich Fromm describes this second phase in the following manner: "The social history of man started with his emerging from a state of oneness with the natural world to an awareness of himself as an entity separate from surrounding nature and men. Yet this awareness remained very dim over long periods of history."[6]

The third phase in the collective life of mankind is the "secondary union" phase. After humanity has traversed its stages of childhood and adolescence, established a positive identity and sense of self, and become wiser and more mature about its place in the universe, it is time to reunite with other human beings and the natural world. In this phase international cooperation, concern for overpopulation, pollution, and the quality of the environment become part of people's conscious and serious concerns. During this phase, solutions to the problems of disunity, disharmony, and violence are also actively sought. Finally, during this phase a new race of humanity emerges to create a new world.

Scientific studies on the origins and evolution of mankind show that close to three million years ago the primitive human began to develop elementary tools for finding and gathering food, indicating the probable beginning of the emergence of humanity from the phase of primary union with the natural world to the phase of separation and individuation. According to Leakey and Lewin: "Ever since the first signs of self-awareness flickered in the minds of our distant ancestors the human (or prehuman) mind has pondered on its relationship with the world outside. We can guess that early humans, say a million or so years ago, were conscious of themselves as an integral part of the environment in which they lived. . . ."[7]

Humanity's self-awareness as an integral part of the environment which it inhabits has its counterpart in contemporary man, in our awareness of the human world in which we live. The natural environment is made up of lakes, trees, animals, natural phenomena, and disaster, while the human world is composed of people, ideas, and biological, sociological, psychological, and spiritual realities. This is the world of creativity, of constant and immensely rapid change, of untold opportunities and dangers, and of body, mind, and soul, and what we now need is to become more aware of those aspects of our own reality which have allowed us to create this world.

The paradox in this situation is that we know more about the creation that surrounds us than we do about our own selves, and this must rank as our most important shortcoming in respect to self-definition, regarding either our responsibilities or our liberties. In this context the Bahá'í concept of liberty and its teachings on the nature of man and the purpose of his life are worthy of serious examination.

The Bahá'í Concept of Liberty

*Struggle for existence is the fountainhead of all
calamities. . . .*
—'Abdu'l-Bahá

From a Bahá'í perspective, true freedom and liberty is achieved when man is "emancipated from the captivity of the world of nature."[8] In other words, true freedom requires the victory of man over his natural instincts and animal-like tendencies, a victory which requires self-knowledge and a motivation and desire for the attainment of whatever is conducive to the exaltation and progress of man. When man lives according to "natural" and instinctual demands, his main concern becomes the struggle for existence which, according to 'Abdu'l-Bahá, is the source of all difficulties and problems in human life and relationships.[9] This view takes us to the first two types of freedom that man has always sought: freedom from the struggle for the necessities of existence and freedom from power struggle and competition with other human beings in order to safeguard one's life and lifestyle.

These forms of freedom are achieved not only through an increase in human knowledge and a greater measure of understanding among people but also, more importantly, through the process of attaining maturity. As a human being matures, he becomes less self-centred and more directed toward the needs and aspirations of others. Freedom from self-centredness and egotism is, therefore, an essential step towards true liberty, achieved when we are more concerned about the needs of others than our own desires, and when we are humble, compassionate, and cooperative rather than proud, aloof, and competitive.

The basis of these concepts is the view that man is a noble being, spiritual in his essence. Although it is true that the functioning of the human body is similar in many ways to that of some animals, nevertheless this resemblance does not prove that man is an animal any more than similarities between some plants and animals prove them to be fundamentally the same. Both the animals and the plants grow, for example, but this similarity does not nullify the enormous differences which exist between them. The case is the same between animal and man, except the difference is even more fundamental and profound.

The assertion of man's essential nobility and spirituality is contrary to the prevailing views of the nature of man and to historical records. Both point to the many occurrences of brutality, violence, greed, and self-centredness shown by man, individually and collectively, behaviour which poses a challenge to the validity of this view.

To respond to this challenge, we need to review the processes and events which, according to Freud, Bettelheim, and other psychological and social scientists, have helped to formulate the prevailing concepts of man's nature and purpose. The blows dealt to man's identity as a unique and noble being (by the Copernican, Darwinian, and Freudian revolutions) were accompanied by painful insights as to the tremendous destructive properties and potential of science and technology when used by man in a misguided manner, as demonstrated during the First and Second World Wars.

An interesting aspect of all these observations is that they focus solely on the biological and psychosocial aspects of human reality, as well as on the physical habitat of man. They fail to see poetry in the universe, and they ignore love found in the lives of men and women, husbands and wives, parents and children, friends, countrymen, and God. They fail to see that the most exciting aspect of a human being is his humanity, rising like a phoenix out of the ashes of his animal dimension.

Humankind is at the crossroads of creation. We belong to the world of matter. The human body is composed of the elements of physical existence; our needs and wants are akin to those of animals; and a human can choose to behave in a way indistinguishable from that of the animals.

However, mankind is also the beginning of the spiritual creation, a created being whose reality transcends matter, a phenomenon constantly observed in everyday life. For example, we are aware of the physical and nonphysical aspects of our love, knowledge, and emotions. The challenge before us is to transcend the limitations of our physical existence and approach more closely the domain of our spiritual reality. The march of mankind through history has been the movement from the physical to the spiritual, from animal to human, but to achieve the highest of these objectives, we must free ourselves from the animalistic bondage of self, from the rule of our instincts and drives, as well as from our ignorance about the true nature of our own being, and, finally, from our own self-centredness, fears, and uncertainties.

'Abdu'l-Bahá comments on the nature of human freedom and liberty in the following manner:

> All creation, preceding Man, is bound by the stern law of nature. The great sun, the multitudes of stars, the oceans and seas, the mountains, the rivers, the trees, and all animals, great or small—none is able to evade obedience to nature's law.
>
> Man alone has freedom, and, by his understanding or intellect, has been able to gain control of and adapt some of those natural laws to his own needs. [10]

Mankind's freedom to control natural laws and create a lifestyle not totally bound by instinctual and natural forces offers choices and alternatives. True liberty is achieved when we have developed a high measure of self-control, discipline, and awareness so that we commit only those acts that reaffirm our individual nobility, reinforce our unity with all other human beings, and contribute to an ever-advancing universal civilization which we must create and towards which we must work.

These objectives can be accomplished when we become aware of the need for unity as the essential requirement of humanity at this juncture in its development. Commenting on the relationship between unity and liberty, Bahá'u'lláh says:

> The fundamental purpose animating the Faith of God and His Religion is to safeguard the interests and promote the unity of the human race, and to foster the spirit of love and fellowship amongst men. Suffer it not to become a source of dissension and discord, of hate and enmity. . . .Whatsoever is raised on this foundation, the changes and chances of the world can never impair its strength, nor will the revolution of countless centuries undermine its structure. . . .Whatsoever passeth beyond the limits of moderation will cease to exert a beneficial influence. Consider for instance such things as liberty, civilization and the like. However much men of understanding may favorably regard them, they will, if carried to excess, exercise a pernicious influence upon men. . . .[11]

Similarly, Bahá'u'lláh asserts that true liberty will be possible only when people begin to live their lives in such a manner that the universal and inevitable processes of the unity of mankind and the spiritualization of the world of humanity can become a reality. He says: "The liberty that profiteth you is to be found nowhere except in complete servitude unto God, the Eternal Truth."[12]

From this perspective, then, one of the prerequisites for the attainment of freedom is the ability of individuals to free themselves from the bondage of their instinctual, material, and animalistic lives and to begin a journey towards enlightenment and spiritualization. Once this process has begun, the second prerequisite for freedom, the recognition of the fundamental oneness of all of humanity, becomes an established fact. This concept dictates that all people receive an equal share of justice and opportunity and that all be helped to develop themselves with dignity and freedom. However, the accomplishment of this objective depends upon yet another important prerequisite, the creation of a new world order where these objectives are attainable.

There is, then, a close relationship between justice, equality, freedom, and peace, as Aurelio Peccei of the Club of Rome notes in the following observation:

> A mass society of 4 or 5 or 6 billion people, a heterogeneous society, made of so many cultures and differentiations within each culture and moreover wielding such a tremendous and growing power, the power of changing completely its habitat, cannot go far if it is not based on a bedrock foundation of justice for all its members. Conditions of inequality, which were acceptable, tolerable or enforceable in the past or even today, are no longer conceivable in the future. Justice is a precondition of everything else. Without justice there cannot be peace or security. There cannot be economic development. Without justice there cannot be freedom, human dignity, quality of life. Society itself runs the risk of ceasing without justice.[13]

The main purpose of justice, however, is to create unity, which is the main prerequisite for the safety and progress of humanity, especially at this point in history. Bahá'u'lláh admonishes:

> The light of men is justice. Quench it not with the contrary winds of oppression and tyranny. The purpose of justice is the appearance of unity among men. . . .O ye men of wisdom among nations! Shut your eyes to estrangement, then fix your gaze upon unity. Cleave tenaciously unto that which will lead to the wellbeing and tranquillity of all mankind. This span of earth is but one homeland and one habitation. It behoveth you to abandon vainglory which causeth alienation and to set your hearts on whatever will ensure harmony.[14]

7

Creating a Technology of Peace

In all matters moderation is desirable. If a thing is carried to excess,
it will prove a source of evil. Consider the civilization of the West, how
it hath agitated and alarmed the peoples of the world. An infernal
engine hath been devised, and hath proved so cruel a weapon of
destruction that its like none hath ever witnessed or heard. The
purging of such deeply-rooted and overwhelming corruptions cannot
be effected unless the peoples of the world unite in pursuit of one
common aim and embrace one universal faith.
—Bahá'u'lláh

Adlai Stevenson once noted, "There is no evil in the atom; only in men's
souls."[1] The truth of this statement lies in the fact that humanity has always
paid more attention to war than to peace. Consequently, mankind is much
more knowledgeable about the nature of war than that of peace; the
scientific community is engaged more in the development of the science
and technology of war than of peace; and the governments of the world are
much more aware of the dynamics of war than those of peace. More
important, the majority of people, the scientific community, and the
leaders of humanity are all convinced that mankind is, by nature, more
inclined toward war than peace. They see war as natural, real, and inevitable, and peace as a fantasy, unnatural, and unobtainable. Due to this

mind-set, many of the resources and efforts of the nations of the world are used to develop the machinery and mechanics of war. While the domain of technology and commerce based on war has expanded to cover almost all important areas of science, industry, and economy, the arena of peace is limited to small bands of people basically engaged in pointing out the evils of war and the need for peace. If we are to change this unfortunate situation and to enhance the development of the technology and infrastructure of peace, we need to develop a better understanding of our spiritual nature and recognize and accept more fully the fact that science and religion are indeed harmonious and not at odds with each other. The development of a technology of peace will be possible only when we have developed a better understanding of our spiritual nature and a fuller recognition and acceptance of the harmony between science and religion.

The Spiritual Nature of Man

O Son of Spirit!
Noble have I created thee, yet thou hast abased thyself.
Rise then unto that for which thou wast created.
  —Bahá'u'lláh

Floyd Matson makes the following observation in his book, *The Idea of Man*: "If it is true, in general, 'that ideas have consequences,' then man's ideas about man have the most far-reaching consequences of all. Upon them may depend the structure of government, the patterns of culture, the purpose of education, the design of the future, and the human or inhuman uses of human beings."[2]

A survey of prevailing concepts of human nature reveals three major concepts: man as animal, man as machine, and man as chosen creation, but with limited options for his destiny. These concepts render man's life meaningless, provide him with little or no purpose, and deprive him of opportunities for growth, enlightenment, and creativity. The spiritual concept of man as defined in the Bahá'í and other spiritual and humanitarian literatures, however, is quite at variance with these views since, from the spiritual perspective, man's power of understanding and his abilities to know, to discover, and to create are the essence of human reality. Thus, a human being possesses a soul with the cardinal capacities of knowledge, love, and will which are all-encompassing in their scope and ever-evolving.

The capacities of knowledge, love, and will, however, do not, in and of themselves, make the life of the individual meaningful, creative, and constructive. For human thoughts to be constructive, they must be focussed on noble aspirations. Just as the thought of war creates war, the thought of peace attracts constructive forces. Likewise, love of war concentrates the human energies of love and will on waging war, while love of peace creates the necessary conditions for the attainment of this long-sought goal of humanity.

'Abdu'l-Bahá states that when man focusses his attention and power of understanding solely on the material issues, the following reactions naturally occur:

> All his aspirations and desires being strengthened by the lower side of the soul's nature, he becomes more and more brutal . . . .Men such as this. . .are entirely without the spirit of Divine compassion, for the celestial quality of the soul has been dominated by that of the material. If, on the contrary, the spiritual nature of the soul has been so strengthened that it holds the material side in subjection, then does the man approach the Divine; his humanity becomes so glorified that the virtues of the Celestial Assembly are manifested in him; he radiates the Mercy of God, he stimulates the spiritual progress of mankind, for he becomes a lamp to show light on their path.[3]

Development of man's spiritual nature, therefore, by definition, is one of the main prerequisites for the establishment of unity and for the attainment of peace. The challenge before us is to begin to study this spiritual nature within a new framework—a major challenge that requires not only the courage to develop a new mind-set but also the humility to accept a new concept of our reality. Quite often fear and pride cause people to wage war. To establish unity and peace, we require the courage and humility to accept our spiritual reality and to focus on the prerequisites for its growth and development. The first prerequisite is a better appreciation of the relationship between one's body and soul. Human reality has two components, the physical and the spiritual. The physical component is the body, while the spiritual component is the rational soul, encompassing the capacity to know, to love, and to will.

Both the physical and spiritual components of human reality are subject to the laws of growth, and both move from their initial primitive simplicity to heights of complexity, from their early limited capacity to great ability and accomplishment. These seemingly parallel and independent processes, however, are in reality neither. First, the growth cycle of the human body, even in its healthiest condition, moves from inability, inefficiency, and incapacity to ability, efficiency, and capacity, and then back to its original weaknesses. Death finally brings an end to all aspects of the body's workings.

The same is not true of man's soul which encompasses the capacity to know, love, and will. Human knowledge moves from a state of ignorance along a path of development in scope, depth, and intensity. Human knowledge never fails to advance, unless the tool necessary for its development, the human brain, is diseased or damaged. Even after death, man's spiritual reality continues its existence in this world, in knowledge and wisdom passed on to the next generations and, in the next world, in the continuing development and refinement of the individual soul (spirit) under different conditions of existence. In the words of psychiatrist Allen Weelis:

> We are carriers of spirit. We know not how nor why nor where. On our shoulders, in our eyes, in anguished hands through unclear realm, into a future unknown, unknowable, and in continual creation, we bear its full weight. Depends it on us utterly, yet we know it not. We inch it forward with each beat of heart, give to it the work of hand, of mind. We falter, pass it on to our children, lay out our bones, fall away, are lost, forgotten. Spirit passes on, enlarged, enriched, more strange, complex.[4]

The second point to be raised about the relationship between the growth of the physical and spiritual components of human reality is that they are totally interdependent at this level of existence. The human body is considered alive as long as the human soul, transmitter of the human power of understanding, knowledge, and awareness, is intact and its qualities are manifested. Consequently, when the human brain, the instrument necessary for the appearance of man's spiritual reality (the soul) in this world, ceases to function, the body is considered dead even though all of its other organs are still functioning and may be used in other bodies through surgical transplant.

Similarly, the human soul (spirit) is dependent on the body in this world and without the body's proper and healthy functioning, development

72

of the power of understanding is hampered. Thus, the body's life is dependent on the soul, and the soul's progress is dependent on the proper functioning of the body. 'Abdu'l-Bahá describes this relationship, in his answer to the question, "What is the wisdom of the spirit's appearing in the body?" saying, in part, the following:

> The wisdom of the appearance of the spirit in the body is this: the human spirit is a Divine Trust and it must traverse all conditions, for its passage and movement through the conditions of existence will be the means of its acquiring perfections . . . .when the human spirit passes through the conditions of existence: it will become the possessor of each degree and station.[5]

'Abdu'l-Bahá further elaborates upon this theme, likening this world to the body and the human being to the soul (spirit):

> If there were no man, the perfections of the spirit would not appear, and the light of the mind would not be resplendent in this world. This world would be like a body without a soul.[6]

The relationship between man and this world has a special bearing on yet another important issue concerning the relationship between body and soul, and that is the manner in which the soul uses the body as an instrument. This process is parallel to the manner in which man uses this world either as his instrument of enlightenment and development or for purposes of brutality and destruction, a process which has a direct bearing on the issue of the development of the technologies of peace and war.

The Computer and the Soul

It is no good taking the right number of atoms and shaking them together with some external energy till they happen to fall into the right pattern, and out drops Adam!
—Paul Davies

One of the most puzzling aspects of the scientific and technological progress of humanity is that so much is used in the service of war. In 1978, 20 billion dollars were spent on finding "new ways to kill man,"[7] and some of this money went to pay 500,000 scientists who are diligently searching for more sophisticated methods to kill.[8] This dedication to the creation of war technology is primarily due to two misconceptions: those concerning the true nature of man and the true nature of the relationship between science and religion.

Since man's true nature is his spiritual reality, his rational soul, or his power of understanding, the human capacity to know, to discover, and to create must rank among the most important properties of the human soul. However, knowledge, discovery, and creativity are neutral in their essence—neither bad nor good, neither destructive nor constructive. Human knowledge and creativity acquire their moral characteristics when they are guided by the spiritual teachings given to mankind periodically and progressively through the appearance of a new prophet or manifestation of God. Thus, the unique personages of Moses, Buddha, Christ, Muhammad, and, most recently, Bahá'u'lláh have brought humanity a wealth of spiritual insights which are the very substance of mankind's moral and ethical heritage and which give the meaning and purpose of life to all individuals.

If the human soul is not guided by these precepts, it becomes solely preoccupied with the material side of life and creates conditions most suitable for the technology of war. 'Abdu'l-Bahá describes this process as follows:

> . . . when man does not open his mind and heart to the blessing of the Spirit, but turns his soul towards the material side, towards the bodily part of his nature, then he is fallen from his high place and he becomes inferior to the inhabitants of the lower animal kingdom. In this case the man is in a sorry plight! For if the spiritual qualities of the soul, open to the breath of the Divine Spirit, are never used, they become atrophied, enfeebled, and at last incapable; whilst the soul's material qualities alone being exercised, they become terribly power-ful—and the unhappy, misguided man becomes more savage, more unjust, more vile, more cruel, more malevolent than the lower animals themselves. . . .Men such as this plan to work evil, to hurt, and to destroy. . . .[9]

This is the condition of our world today. Many governments and scientists are engaged in activities which cause evil, hurt, and destruction — conditions which impelled Aurelio Peccei, in 1974, to observe:

Our nations, instead of uniting in a supreme effort, are still egocentric and antagonistic with each other and busy arming and trading in all sorts of weapons. You know that the nuclear stockpiles, already in existence, pack so much explosive [power] that they can wipe out mankind in a few hours. Each one of us has, in those stockpiles, an endowment of TNT or ordinary explosives equal to 12 tons. This is sheer madness. But it is only the reflection of the moral disorder and disintegration of a society which invests, every year, some of its best scientific and political energies and between 6 and 8% of the total world product in perfecting the doctrines, the technologies, the armaments of extermination. This is a society in which the tragic irony exists that we trust security in what, using a trade word in defence circles, is called M.A.D. (mutual, assured destruction).[10]

The human rational soul, however, once enlightened by spiritual teachings, can then reconcile the supposedly irreconcilable realities of science and religion, creating a new technology of peace. In order to comprehend more fully the concept of the development of such a technology, we must return to the issue of man's spiritual nature.

To recapitulate, the fundamental faculties of the soul are knowledge, love, and will, which, although nonphysical in essence, are nevertheless dependent on physical instruments to manifest themselves in this life. Thus, a thought or an idea can be transmitted only through physical faculties and instruments such as speaking, writing, visual demonstrations, and tactile and other sensory modalities. Likewise, love is shown through touch, sight, speech, cooperative activities, and a host of other processes, all of which depend on the use of the body. The same is true of human will.

In addition, man invents instruments and objects to extend and even surpass the potential of different parts of his body. Thus, through the power of his soul, he creates machines which allow him to fly, to move swiftly, to handle the most minute objects, and to perform other physical feats which would not otherwise be in his capacity. For example, man, with his knowledge and his power of understanding, not only sees and studies objects with his eyes, but expands the capacity of his eyes by inventing the microscope, the telescope, the television, satellites, and other instruments that allow him to see deeper, farther, and more clearly. The same extension of human capabilities occurs with other inventions which broaden the scope of human capacity for hearing, touch, smell, and taste.

However, of all man's inventions, the most interesting and significant are those which facilitate and extend the work of his brain, the seat and the main instrument of his soul. Here I am referring to all machines and instruments which perform mathematical and logical functions hitherto performed by only the most educated people. As an extension of the human brain the computer is, therefore, another very important adjunct to the human body which, as a whole, functions as a tool for the human soul. It would be folly if we were to see machines and other human inventions as anything but extensions of the physical reality of man, which, in turn, is meaningful and alive only if it is quickened, influenced, and directed by the human power of understanding, the human soul. If man decides, through perversity, to abdicate power and control over his inventions, then he devalues the world of life to the mechanistic, meaningless, and destructive movement of machines.

Harmony of Science and Religion

From every second or third house came the voices of people buried and abandoned, who invariably screamed, with formal politeness, "Tasukete Kure! Help, if you please!" The priests recognized several ruins from which these cries came as the homes of friends, but because of the fire it was too late to help.
—John Hersey

A woman who looked like an expectant mother was dead. At her side, a girl of about three years of age brought some water in an empty can she had found. She was trying to let her mother drink from it.
—Described by Kikuno Segawa

. . . it is quite true that Aga Mirza Ashraf of Abade was put to death for his religion in the most barbarous manner in Isfahan about October last. The hatred of the Mullas was not satisfied with his murder, but they mutilated the poor body publicly in the Maidan in the most savage manner, and then burnt what was left of it.
—Edward G. Browne

76

These quotations graphically demonstrate the destructive effects resulting from the abuse of both science and religion. To prevent such an outcome, there is a need for the creation of a technology of peace. The main prerequisite for this technology is unity, specifically that of science and religion. This concept goes beyond conditions of coexistence and tolerance which are, so far, the closest relationship reached between science and religion. Historically, these two areas of human knowledge and experience have been, at worst, hostile, and, at best, mutually tolerant. The battle between clergy and scientists is paralleled in individual lives in the form of struggles between heart and head, emotion and reason, faith and logic, and subjectivity and objectivity.

However, defining reality and formulating a purpose for life are among the most important functions of both science and religion. Science has the physical world as its object of study and, consequently, perceives the world according to the laws governing matter. When carried out alone, without spiritual reality, science creates a religion of its own called materialism. Frederick Turner describes this phenomenon in the following manner:

> In about 1600 a new religion, materialism, appears on the scene. Its practice is what we usually call economic activity and its higher emotions include a sense of the beauty of nature and awe at its workings, and a sense of triumph in technological achievement. Its technology is atomistic: like God, the atom of matter is indivisible, eternal, invulnerable, responsible for all events in the world. Unlike God, though, it is not conscious or personal . . . . [11]

Turner elaborates upon some of materialism's most important characteristics and points out that explanations of the "complex and ambiguous behaviour of the world" become more "concrete and unambiguous"[12] as we analyze our world in the simple terms of atomic events.

Analysis, by its very nature, is a process of separating, breaking up, and loosening. It endeavours to break up complex phenomena into simple parts and to formulate laws governing the interrelationship of these constituent parts. Materialism is a good example of such a reductionist approach to life and existence. The fundamental and dangerous flaw of such an approach is that it explains all reality according to the main characteristics of atoms of matter, in terms such as "impersonality," "insentience," and "unintelligence."[13] In contrast, synthesis is the process of combining parts into a whole and of uniting elements or thoughts to make them more complete and connected. It is, therefore, akin to creativity and allows for the understanding of a phenomenon in its state of wholeness, not merely by analysis of its component parts.

In the contemporary materialistic world, analysis is the main approach to understanding both science and religion. There is currently a profound fascination with analysis at all levels and in all fields of human existence, with the consequence that we know much more about the component parts than we do about the whole. We know more about memory, learning, cognition, and the biological changes accompanying emotions than we know about the human soul, and we also have more information about the practices, dogmas, and doctrines of the different sects of various religions and denominations than we do about spirituality and a spiritual way of life. Our knowledge of the distribution of minerals, farmlands, pollution, and armaments in a given country is much more complete than our knowledge of the conditions of human life in the same area. In short, we know a lot about material things, human physiology and biology included, but very little about the whole picture of life and existence in general.

Systems Theory attempts to create a holistic approach to all phenomena, as do schools of thought such as the ancient philosophy of the Chinese and the Buddhist approach to life. However, these efforts must become far more integrated and comprehensive if they are to bring about a creative and unified approach to the definition of reality and life. This "new vision of reality," as Capra observes, must be "based on awareness of the essential interrelatedness and interdependence of all phenomena—physical, biological, psychological, social, and cultural."[14]

Capra, in his enumeration of "all phenomena," fails to mention the spiritual phenomenon. No doubt, by including psychological, social, and cultural phenomena, he has taken into account some aspects of spiritual reality; however, this is not sufficient. We must acknowledge spiritual reality and endeavour to understand its nature. This reality creates a condition of unity at all levels of human experience and knowledge, harmonizes the processes of analysis and synthesis, unites the two realities of science and religion, and, in so doing, helps humanity to understand itself and to develop its world. In 'Abdu'l-Bahá's words:

> Religion and science are the two wings upon which man's
> intelligence can soar into the heights, with which the human

soul can progress. It is not possible to fly with one wing alone! Should a man try to fly with the wing of religion alone he would quickly fall into the quagmire of superstition, whilst on the other hand, with the wing of science alone he would also make no progress, but fall into the despairing slough of materialism. . . . When religion shorn of its superstitions, traditions, and unintelligent dogmas, shows its conformity with science, then will there be a great unifying, cleansing force in the world which will sweep before it all wars, disagreements, discords and struggles—and then will mankind be united in the power of the Love of God.[15]

This statement indicates that it is through the harmony of science and religion that we can create a technology of peace. Science alone provides us, at best, with the technology to build. Building is an act of construction, a bringing together of materials to erect a structure or assemble a machine, and while buildings and machines are useful tools, they are lifeless. At their best, they serve man to create a material civilization while, at their worst, they help man to wage wars and commit acts of destruction.

Religion alone, without the benefit of science, at best creates a community with its own hierarchy and power structure, with divisions between believers and nonbelievers, clergy and layman, sinful and saved. At its worst, religion fosters superstition, prejudice, disunity, hatred, and bloodshed.

Einstein comments on the relationship between science and religion in this manner:

Science can only be created by those who are thoroughly imbued with the aspirations toward truth and understanding. This source of feeling, however, springs from the sphere of religion. To this there also belongs the faith in the possibility that the regulations valid for the world of existence are rational; that is comprehensible to reason. I cannot conceive of a genuine scientist without that profound faith. The situation may be expressed by an image: science without religion is lame, religion without science is blind.[16]

Only through the harmonious and united functioning of religion and science are we able to transform the building capacities of science and the quickening powers of religion into creativity, allowing us to unite, and to make possible a technology of peace. However, harmony of science and religion is not sufficient for the development of a united and harmonized world; in addition, there is a need for the continuing progress of both religion and science. Science, through the scientific method, is in a constant state of change and progress, with its ultimate aim the discovery of unified laws which will uncover further mysteries of nature. Therefore, a true scientist is always in search of the laws of unity governing the world of creation. Jacob Bronowski comments on the scientist's search for unity in his enumeration of some of Einstein's most important discoveries. He says: "So in a lifetime Einstein joined light to time, and time to space; energy to matter, matter to space, and space to gravitation. At the end of his life, he was still working to seek a unity between gravitation and the forces of electricity and magnetism."[17]

The same principles should and do apply to religion which, like science, should be progressive, evolving, and unifying. 'Abdu'l-Bahá describes the need for the harmonious progress of science and religion in the following manner:

Religion is the outer expression of the divine reality. Therefore it must be living, vitalized, moving and progressive. If it be without motion and non-progressive it is without the divine life; it is dead. The divine institutes are continuously active and evolutionary; therefore the revelation of them must be progressive and continuous. All things are subject to re-formation. This is a century of life and renewal. Sciences and arts, industry and invention have been reformed. Law and ethics have been reconstituted, reorganized. The world of thought has been regenerated. Sciences of former ages and philosophies of the past are useless today. Present exigencies demand new methods of solution; world problems are without precedent. Old ideas and modes of thought are fast becoming obsolete. Ancient laws and archaic ethical systems will not meet the requirements of modern conditions, for this is clearly the century of a new life, the century of the revelation of the reality and therefore the greatest of all centuries. Consider how the scientific developments of fifty years have surpassed and eclipsed the knowledge and achievements of all the former ages combined. Would the announcements and theories of ancient astronomers explain our present knowledge of the sun-worlds and planetary systems?

Would the mask of obscurity which beclouded mediaeval centuries meet the demand for clear-eyed vision and understanding which characterizes the world today? Will the despotism of former governments answer the call for freedom which has risen from the heart of humanity in this cycle of illumination? It is evident that no vital results are now forthcoming from the customs, institutions and standpoints of the past. In view of this, shall blind imitations of ancestral forms and theological interpretations continue to guide and control the religious life and spiritual development of humanity today? Shall man gifted with the power of reason unthinkingly follow and adhere to dogma, creeds and hereditary beliefs which will not bear the analysis of reason in this century of effulgent reality? Unquestionably this will not satisfy men of science, for when they find premise or conclusion contrary to present standards of proof and without real foundation, they reject that which has been formerly accepted as standard and correct and move forward from new foundations.[18]

Harmony of science and religion, once achieved, will create in our societies remarkable conditions of creativity, life, and unity which, in turn, will hasten the advent of mankind's age of maturity. Under these circumstances, our noble and spiritual natures will become more fully developed, and we will be able to create a peaceful world such as we cannot fully describe at the present time. Hence, we have the notion that the concepts of nobility, spirituality, unity, and peace belong to the realms of Utopia and not reality. But Utopia—the imaginary and remote place of ideal perfection—is, by virtue of mankind's coming of age, becoming more realistic, a place of growth and creativity towards which we are slowly advancing.

Part Three:

Peace and the New World Order

8

Peace and the New World Order:
Reality or Utopia?

*So we saunter toward the Holy Land, till one day the sun shall shine
more brightly than ever has done, shall perchance shine into our
minds and hearts, and light up our whole lives with a great awakening
light, as warm and serene and golden as on a bankside in autumn.*
—Henry David Thoreau

In the previous two parts I have attempted to show that the quest for peace
alone is not sufficient for the achievement of world peace and that peace is
an elusive objective and will remain so until we begin to focus our energies
on the attainment of its prerequisites. Although at first glance the range and
magnitude of these prerequisites for peace are overwhelming, a closer look
will show that all are closely related to the issue of unity and that there exists
a unity paradigm with unique characteristics and conditions.

The unity paradigm is an all-encompassing concept, at the same time
simple and complex, individual and universal, concrete and abstract,
emotional and intellectual, material and spiritual. The paradigm of unity
challenges us to look at ourselves in new ways and to reappraise our
previously-held conceptions in the light of this new perspective on human
reality.

85

In this third part I will attempt to review the related issues of human disunity and human violence from the perspective of the unity paradigm. I have chosen these two specific issues because they are at the root of war and our difficulty in achieving peace. The concept of unity is dealt with extensively in Bahá'í thought; therefore, a critical evaluation of the Bahá'í perspective on unity and peace will be helpful in this discussion. I have also included in this section two other chapters, one dealing with the Bahá'í community as a contemporary example of the unity paradigm and the other a review of the emerging new world order.

The Bahá'í perspective on peace, with its focus on humanity's coming of age and the establishment of unity within the framework of an enlightened, just, and spiritually-oriented world order, could be perceived by many observers as incongruous with the realities of both the past and present. These observers state that such a perspective is utopian and ignores painful realities. They point out that throughout history mankind has been enamored of war and little inclined towards peace. They also point to the fact that scientific and technological developments have increased both the destructiveness and the frequency of wars and have dramatically demonstrated our capacity for violence. Finally, they argue that the present condition of the world, divided and burdened with awesome quantities of lethal weapons, is a living testimony to humanity's failure to make any meaningful progress towards peace. These issues need to be answered if a case is to be made for the feasibility of a peaceful world.

Human Disunity: A Reappraisal

The inhabitants of the earth are divided not only by race, nation, religion or ideology, but also, in a sense, by their position in time.
—Alvin Toffler

The story of mankind's disunity is also that of its unity. In its march toward maturity, humanity has achieved many remarkable acts of unity, such as the successive creation of family, clan, tribe, state, and nation. Humanity has also achieved a greater degree of understanding and empathy among various races and ethnic groups, and we have seen the powerful contemporary movement for achieving equality between men and women, the

86

remarkable increase in world consciousness concerning the need for a new world order, and, finally, the creation of multinational organizations and world agencies as first steps towards the achievement of unity. These accomplishments have contributed to the collective growth of humanity, helping mankind to arrive at its present stage of development. However, these are limited unities, no longer appropriate for the needs of humanity today. The emergence of a global society and a united world demand wider unity, the absence of which has made all other types of unity inoperative and even dangerous. In one of his talks on unity, after describing a number of lesser unities, such as those of language, nationhood, and political affiliation, 'Abdu'l-Bahá points out:

> From these limited unities mentioned only limited outcomes proceed whereas unlimited unity produces unlimited result. For instance, from the limited unity of race or nationality the results at most are limited. It is like a family living alone and solitary; there are no unlimited or universal outcomes from it.
>
> The unity which is productive of unlimited results is first a unity of mankind. . . .[1]

World unity is not a utopian concept based on hope. It is, rather, a natural outcome of the collective growth and progress of humanity and is as inevitable as is the progression of the individual from childhood through adolescence to adulthood and maturity. Today, humanity is ready for such a challenge. Once again, 'Abdu'l-Bahá's explanation of this fact is illuminating:

> In cycles gone by, though harmony was established, yet, owing to the absence of means, the unity of all mankind could not have been achieved. Continents remained widely divided, nay even among the peoples of one and the same continent association and interchange of thought were wellnigh impossible. Consequently, intercourse, understanding and unity amongst all the peoples and kindreds of the earth were unattainable. In this day, however, means of communication have multiplied, and the five continents of the earth have virtually merged into one. . . .In like manner all the members of the human family, whether peoples or governments, cities or villages, have become increasingly interdependent. For none is self-sufficiency any longer possible, inasmuch as political ties unite all peoples and nations, and

the bonds of trade and industry, of agriculture and education, are being strengthened every day. Hence the unity of all mankind can in this day be achieved.[2]

This reappraisal challenges us to concentrate our efforts on the goal of attaining the unity of mankind, rather than exaggerating its differences and conflicts. Unity is a multidimensional phenomenon involving aspects such as thought, language, politics, and racial and national distinctions. In his discussion of the "seven candles of unity," 'Abdu'l-Bahá identifies those unities which must be established in order to achieve world unity. They are unity of government, thought, freedom, religion, nations, races, and language.[3] The order in which these unities are to be achieved is not identified, but a cursory study shows that initial attempts at establishing these various types of unity have already been made, and considerable progress has been achieved in some areas. The challenge before us now is to identify and intensify these forces and to refrain from activating the processes of further disunity. As Leakey and Lewin comment:

> It is a truism to say that politics are international. But this being so, it follows that any attempt to achieve long-term stability for humanity can come only through a global determination and will. It is not our intention to suggest how global politics might be run, with a world government or whatever other machinery might be appropriate. Rather, we wish to suggest that unless there is an acceptance of the oneness of the human race, a real spirit of brotherhood, then the political machinery, however sophisticated, will grind to a halt. The deep human drive for cooperation lends itself to achieve that aim. Just as human propensity for group cooperation has in the past been harnessed to wage war between nations, it is now imperative that the same basic drive be channeled into a global effort to rescue humanity from itself.[4]

This and similar calls for a new world order by various political, scientific, academic, religious, and other leaders are not merely expressions of hope or desperate responses to the mounting crises in respect to war. They are, rather, responses to the fact that the era of the oneness of mankind and the time for establishment of a new world order are finally at hand, and the necessary prerequisites for their ultimate achievement are already in operation. As Shoghi Effendi observes, the oneness of mankind ". . .represents the consummation of human evolution—an evolution that has had its earliest beginnings in the birth of family life, its subsequent development in the achievement of tribal solidarity, leading in turn to the constitution of the city-state, and expanding later into the institution of independent and sovereign nations."[5]

This review of human history from the perspective of the unity paradigm removes one of the most difficult obstacles for the achievement of unity: the strongly-held view that unity in diversity, as proposed in Bahá'í thought, is not possible. To address this challenging issue we need to define the concept of diversity used in Bahá'í literature. If by diversity is meant differences and inequalities in respect to such fundamental issues as human nobility, integrity, and rights and opportunities, then it follows that unity in diversity is an impossible task to achieve. This kind of unity is only possible when there is an unconditional comprehension and acceptance of the fact that at the very core of our humanity we are one and the same. That is, we are all noble and loving individuals, but we are capable of learning to manifest our nobility and to love in a unique manner; hence our diversity. This is not diversity in respect to our fundamental humanity and interests. At the level of our humanness and human interests we are all the same. We all desire to love and to be loved, wish to know and be known. In this sense all humanity is yearning for the same things, but as individuals we follow our quest in a manner unique to each of us. This process is at the core of beauty, creativity, and richness of both human individuals and human societies.

The politics of power and domination so prevalent in the history of the world and so influential in the nature of the unfoldment of human civilization thus far are characteristics of childhood and adolescent stages of growth. They are valid as long as we live and function at that stage of development but, with the advent of humanity's coming of age, struggle for power and domination will of necessity give way to the forces of mutual strength, equality, and cooperation. All the accomplishments of humanity are due to the ability of humans to cooperate and create, not to compete and destroy. It is this perspective of history that gives us cause to be optimistic and to state with certainty that the age of oneness and unity has arrived. However, to establish unity we need more than awareness, enthusiasm, and motivation. We also need know-how. It is clear that to create a new level of unity, there is a need for a fresh approach to the resolution of human conflicts—an approach which not only opposes but also transcends violence and disunity, and in doing so, conquers them.

9

A Symptom not a Disease:
A New Perspective on Violence

Thoughts of war bring destruction to all harmony, well-being, restfulness and content. Thoughts of love are constructive of brotherhood, peace, friendship and happiness. . . .

If you desire with all your heart friendship with every race on earth, your thought, spiritual and positive, will spread; it will become the desire of others, growing stronger and stronger, until it reaches the minds of all men.

Do not despair! Work steadily, sincerely and love will conquer hate.
    —'Abdu'l-Bahá

Some day, after mastering the winds, the waves, the tides and the gravity, we will harness for God the energies of love. And then for the second time in the history of the world, man will have discovered fire.
    —Pierre Teilhard de Chardin

Violence is a worldwide phenomenon affecting people of all ages, backgrounds, and conditions: the young and the old, the poor and the helpless, minorities and women, intellectuals and artists. While violence may be the result of ignorance, emotional illness, or self-defence, the majority of violent acts are deliberate and premeditated. They are cloaked in the garment of love for one's family, religion, nation, or race, and are performed in the name of honour, freedom, democracy, progress, and God. Regardless of these explanations and justifications, human violence remains the most alarming indication of humanity's failure to free itself from the bondage of instinctual, self-centred, and immature life. Mankind is still too fascinated with its childhood world of make-believe and adolescent bravado to accept the responsibility of freedom.

These facts notwithstanding, the age of maturity is approaching, and the health of humanity depends on people preparing to live a life according to the mature laws of cooperation, other-directedness, selflessness, and service. In order to achieve these objectives, we must develop new approaches to human violence and, ultimately, prevent its occurrence. Towards this end, it would be helpful to review some of the more common responses of people and nations towards violence.

A very common response, especially when violence does not touch us directly, is to ignore it. An example of this is the generally indifferent response of people towards news of violence in other parts of the world, especially if those affected are of a different race, nationality, religion, or background. Such a response indicates our inability or refusal to accept the oneness of mankind, as well as the fact that violence against one is violence against all. While violence is frightening and many people naturally wish to avoid such an experience, both avoidance and denial that violence is occurring are effective only temporarily and are basically acts of self-delusion.

A second common response to violence is to rationalize its occurrence, an approach particularly prevalent in the biological, psychological, and sociological theories of aggression and violence. Every violent act is seen, in the last analysis, as a natural, understandable, and even acceptable response to certain psychological or social stresses and events or specific biological imperatives. Therefore, theories abound on the instinctual, territorial, physiological, behavioural, and environmental roots of violence. However, these theories and explanations do not offer a plan for the eradication of war and violence and, at best, suggest coping techniques and deterring practices. Konrad Lorenz offers the following remedies for human violence, based on his extensive work on aggression:

> The first, the most obvious and the most important precept is
> . . . 'know thyself': we must deepen our insight into the causal
> concatenations governing our own behaviour. . . .One line is the

92

objective, ethological investigation of all the possibilities of discharging aggression in its primal form on substitute objects. . . .The second is the psycho-analytical study of so-called sublimation. . . .The third way of avoiding aggression. . .is the promotion of personal acquaintance and, if possible, friendship between individual members of different ideologies or nations. The fourth and perhaps the most important measure to be taken immediately is the intelligent and responsible channelling of militant enthusiasm. . . .[1]

It is clear that Lorenz considers human aggression to be a natural and unavoidable phenomenon which needs to be discharged against objects other than human beings, sublimated in the form of activities which satisfy the human need for aggressive behaviour, and decreased, if possible, by encouraging friendship. Finally, in his opinion, the militant enthusiasm of our youth should be channelled by finding genuine causes that are worth serving in the modern world.[2]

The third and by far the most common response to violence is violence itself. In our world today, responding to violence with a greater degree of violence is considered the main solution to the problem while at the same time all indications point to the futility of such an approach. The proponents of such a reaction obviously do not realize that one cannot remedy a disease by prescribing more of the pathogen causing it. These and other solutions, such as those proposed by Lorenz as well as other experts on human violence, including the creation of balance of power and politics of deterrence, are pathetically inadequate when compared with the intensity and scope of human violence. Wars mankind has waged, atrocities committed in the concentration camps and prison yards, brutalities inflicted upon human beings in political, ideological, and religious interrogation and indoctrination centres, and, finally, the coldblooded maiming and murder of multitudes by modern instruments of death such as the bombs dropped on Hiroshima and Nagasaki and the napalm poured on people in more recent wars, cannot be stopped by these conceptually and tactically inadequate solutions. We need a radically different approach to the solution of human violence. Our mind-set has to change, and our understanding of both human nature and human violence has to be altered drastically. It is in this light that the following responses to violence merit our considered attention.

Apart from the most common responses to human violence, such as ignoring, rationalizing, or combatting violence with violence—all of which are considered to be natural and essential for self-protection—we have a few examples of a radically different and effective approach in the form of the nonviolence movement. We see, notably, the work of Mahatma Gandhi in South Africa and India, and Martin Luther King in the United States. To a less dramatic degree, we have the example of Ferenc Deak, a Catholic landowner in Hungary who, in the mid-nineteenth century, mobilized the Hungarian people in a peaceful and nonviolent manner against the immense powers of Emperor Franz Josef of Austria. Finally, we can examine the nonviolent but courageous stand of the King of Denmark against the Nazi invaders, and the dramatic nonviolent stand of the Norwegian teachers against the horrendous brutality perpetrated against them by the Nazi soldiers. All these examples point to the effective results of the nonviolence movement.

Richard Gregg, in his classic book, *The Power of Nonviolence*, points out that when we respond to violence with violence, we in essence justify the violent act of the attacker. If we respond with nonviolence, then we create a kind of moral jiu-jitsu, to paraphrase Gregg, a situation in which the lack of physical opposition by the user of psychic jiu-jitsu causes the attacker to lose his moral balance.

Gregg describes the attitude of the nonviolent person in the following manner:

> He does not respond to the attacker's violence with counter-violence. Instead, he accepts the blows good-temperedly, stating his belief as to the truth of the matter in dispute, asking for an examination of both sides of the dispute, and stating his readiness to abide by the truth. He offers resistance, but only in moral terms. He states his readiness to prove his sincerity by his own suffering rather than by inflicting suffering on the assailant. He accepts blow after blow, showing no signs of fear or resentment, keeping steadily good-humored and kindly in look of eye, tone of voice, and posture of body and arms. To violence he opposes nonviolent resistance.[3]

In this passage Gregg, who observed Gandhi first-hand in India and dedicated much of his life to the study of the nonviolence movement, focusses on the ideal manner in which a nonviolent resister will oppose violence. He puts forward several examples of successful nonviolent

94

approaches recorded throughout history and particularly in this century as a proof both of the effectiveness and the viability of such a method. While the foregoing description of nonviolence focusses on the individual, principles of non-violence can also be applied to groups of people and nations. Bertrand Russell, during the First World War, made the following statement in respect to national application of the nonviolence principles:

> Passive resistance, if it were adopted deliberately by the will of the whole nation, with the same measure of courage and discipline which is now displayed, might achieve a far more perfect protection for what is good in national life than armies and navies can ever achieve, without demanding the carnage and waste and welter of brutality involved in modern war.[4]

There is ample evidence that methods of nonviolence have been successful both at the individual and collective levels and that the main advantages of the nonviolence approach are its moral and psychological powers. The nonviolent individual, when facing violence, responds unexpectedly. He creates surprise and doubt in the attackers, attracts the attention of other people, arouses deep feelings of empathy and sympathy, especially when suffering and sacrifice are involved, and, above all, addresses himself to the humanity and fundamental goodness of all people, including both the victim and the oppressor. Such a nonviolence movement creates conditions which render aggression and violence ineffective and cause the attacker(s) to capitulate and accept defeat. However, the long-term effectiveness of the nonviolence movement has at best been marginal. There are several reasons for this. To begin with, as Gregg observes, unity is an essential condition for the success of nonviolence, and therefore, in the absence of unity, the successes of the nonviolence movement have been dramatic, but limited and short-lived:

> Violence is based upon fear and anger and uses them to the utmost. . . .these two emotions are based on the idea of separation, of division. Nonviolent resistance, on the other hand, is based upon the idea of unity. The hypothesis of nonviolent resisters is that the strongest factor in human beings, in the long run, is their unity—that they have more in common as a human family than as separate individuals.[5]

Another reason for the short-lived effectiveness of nonviolent resistance is that nonviolence does not have a force of its own and, consequently, cannot be effective on an ongoing basis. In essence, nonviolence needs violence in order to have any influence on human society. However, a violent world even where nonviolent resistance is victorious is not synonymous with a peaceful and creative world.

When compared with the alternatives of ignoring violence, countering it with further violence, or rationalizing it away, the concept of nonviolence emerges as the most viable option, but at the same time, it is clear that the nonviolence movement has been only partially successful even among those who have benefitted most from it. It is this perplexing and discouraging fact that impels us to search for another, more effective approach to deal with violence and eventually prevent its occurrence. We need to transcend violence. In this process, we can release the vast creative energies which are now being wasted in countering violence. To achieve this objective, we need first to reevaluate our definition and, thus, our understanding of violence.

The dictionary definition of violence describes a process in which a person suffers physical or emotional injury and hurt as a result of a forceful and destructive event, normally committed by another person. As such, therefore, violence is a phenomenon which we all experience under certain conditions and consequently acquire first-hand knowledge in respect to its effects on ourselves and others. One would expect that we would have learned more about an experience so universal in its occurrence and so personal in its effects.

Throughout history, the human qualities of exploration and inquisitiveness have enabled us to learn much about ourselves and our world, and usually we have been able to acquire considerable insight into the conditions which have been most universally bothersome to us. Many attempts have been made at discovering the roots of violence and finding ways to prevent it. However, in spite of these facts we have failed miserably. As mankind has evolved and become more capable of preventing many unhealthy and unacceptable conditions of life, it seems that man has also become less capable of preventing or even controlling occurrences of violence. In fact, so far in this century we have committed more violent acts than all those previously recorded throughout history. This condition is most alarming and makes it imperative that we focus on the issue of violence from a totally different perspective. Towards this end, I would like to put forward the concept that violence is merely a symptom of a more serious underlying social disease—disunity. Or to put it differently, violence exists when unity is absent. Therefore, the study of violence alone will not give necessary insights for its prevention. Rather, we need to eradicate the underlying disease of disunity in order to free ourselves from violence, and this is only possible through the creation of conditions of unity in human society.

The challenge of perceiving violence as the absence of unity is enormous. It calls for a remarkable change in our mind-set, our concept of good and evil, our view of friends and enemies, our understanding of ourselves and, ultimately, our understanding of reality. If violence is indeed merely a symptom and not the disease itself, then it is no wonder that our attempts at controlling and preventing it have failed.

There is a parallel between violence and illness. If illness is defined as absence of health, then our efforts will be primarily focussed on the promotion of health by appropriate nutrition, an optimal level of activity, purification of the environment from natural and chemical noxious agents which weaken or destroy our health, the avoidance of alcohol and other agents such as tobacco, and, finally, by the adoption of a lifestyle which is moderate, purposeful, joyous, and free from undue stress. These factors are all health-promoting and thus preventative in nature. They are economical, pleasant, and not destructive. However, because we have poor nutrition, immoderate levels of activity and inactivity, and we continue to pollute our environment and live an immoderate, highly stressful life, we have become burdened with serious and chronic diseases. Furthermore, in our attempts to deal with consequences of these conditions, we have created an expensive and highly complex medical industry which is becoming increasingly inadequate. Ultimately, a change in our perspective on disease and health will help to put our energies into the prevention of disease, which will improve the contemporary situation regarding health and illness. Likewise in respect to violence, we are suffering from both individual and collective lifestyles which are based on distrust, competition, self-centredness, inequality, injustice, separation, and disunity. Such conditions are fertile grounds for the development of violence. If we are to create a violence-free society, we must, above all, realize that such a society must be not only free from violence, but also endowed with the life-engendering and creative forces of unity.

This redefinition of violence, therefore, dictates that in the face of violence, the most effective tools with which to counter it are love and affirmation of the unity between the oppressed and the oppressor. On the surface this is a most unrealistic proposition. In the face of violent attack by those who are intent to harm or kill, it seems bizarre and simplistic to ask not only for nonviolence but also for kindness and love based on the idea of human unity. One could easily imagine that under these circumstances the victims would be annihilated. One may even point to such historical events as the holocaust for the proof of this assertion. However, before we reject this particular approach, let us again look at the phenomenon of violence.

Most students of human violence assert that both the aggressors and the victims of violence, especially the aggressors, are filled with fear and mistrust: They are afraid of everyone and everything, but particularly of themselves. Jean-Paul Sartre, in his evaluation of the anti-Semite, gives special attention to the role of fear in human violence:

> We are now in a position to understand the anti-Semite. He is a man who is afraid not of Jews, to be sure, but of himself, of his own consciousness, of his liberty, of his instincts, of his responsibilities, of solitariness, of change, of society and of the world, of everything, except the Jews.[6]

This fear becomes enormously destructive when combined with the view that human nature is violent in its essence, that some people are created more violent than others, and that the ultimate method to achieve our objectives is through the use of force within a competitive framework.

Fear and anger are always mixed, and when one predominates, the other is barely below the surface and will manifest itself with the slightest provocation. When an aggressor and a potential victim come face to face, they will be highly prone to violent interaction if they deal with one another from the perspectives of fear, anger, mistrust, and dislike. However, if one of them begins to respond from the perspective of courage, calmness, trust, and a genuine sense of solidarity with and liking for the other person, a different dynamic emerges. Obviously under these circumstances, it is the victim who has to have the courage to respond to violence in this new manner.

In doing so, the victim helps decrease both the fear and anger of the aggressor by not responding with fear or anger himself. More important, by focussing on the basic humanity of his aggressor, such a victim gives a potent reminder to the aggressor about the fundamental unity which exists between them. This is so because at the core of all human beings and in the very essence of human reality resides an ongoing quest for higher levels of love, enlightenment, peacefulness, and intimacy. Humanity, by definition, is based on the forces of creativity and life and not on those of destructiveness and death, and the process of becoming human is that of evolving in respect to our capacities to know, love, and create. All human beings, even those who seem totally violent and destructive, are nonetheless greatly responsive to the powerful forces of love, care, and kindness. An example of this phenomenon is the tenderness and love for family, children, and friends displayed by some of the most destructive and violent persons in history. Except for a few very unhealthy and exceptionally pathological individuals, people in general are drawn to love, unity, and creativity by the forces of their humanness.

When a victim of violence responds with courage and displays love and care, he is directing himself to the humanness of his oppressor and automatically reaffirming his essential unity with his aggressor. While this process is initiated and carried out with a deliberate and well thought-out plan by the victim, its effects on the oppressor usually take place at subconscious or unconscious levels, and as a consequence the aggressor's behaviour towards such a victim becomes lenient without his conscious awareness. That is one reason why those individuals who have responded to human cruelty with love have had such a remarkable influence on the course of history and have been such enduring examples for people throughout the ages. The life histories of the founders of the major religions, such as Abraham, Buddha, Christ, and Bahá'u'lláh, as well as the lives of some of their followers, provide excellent examples of this new response to violence. However, these responses have, throughout history, occurred on an individual basis. At this stage in the history of humanity, we are, for the first time, capable of acting in this manner on a collective basis, creating a global civilization whose actions transcend violence.

Acts of love, courage, and kindness have at least two direct effects. First, they affect the oppressors by touching their humanness and piercing the many barriers existing between the oppressor and the victim, ultimately reaching to the domain of their essential unity as members of the human family. The second effect of these acts is on all other people who, although not participating in the drama of the oppressor and the victim, are neverthe-less touched by the potency of the affirmative response of such victims to aggression. In essence, the courage and humanity of these victims reaffirm the courage and humanity of all people and remind us that the direction of our movement in life is towards love, life, and unity. While responding to violence with forces of love and unity is extremely dramatic and fundamen-tally more effective than a violent and aggressive response, nevertheless the greatest value of this new concept lies in its universal application. In other words, the forces of love, care, and unity should become the modus operandi of society, so that the occurrence of violence will decrease and eventually stop.

It is neither sufficient nor judicious to wait for violence to occur in order to respond with an active display of love and care. Rather, we must create a new society, a new world order in which the forces of love and unity are operative at all times and under all conditions. In order to understand the dynamics of this specific approach to violence, we should study its use and effectiveness in a relatively accessible and contemporary setting, so that the data obtained will be verifiable and the qualities of the individuals and communities involved open to research and evaluation. Examples of this nature are difficult to find, and consequently we are limited in our choices. The Bahá'í community of Iran is perhaps the first and only relatively large community which has adopted this approach to the prevention and resolution of human violence. Thus, its case merits close attention and in-depth study.

10

Violence Disarmed: A Contemporary Example

Crito: . . .*Nor can I think that you are justified, Socrates, in betraying your own life when you might be saved; this is playing into the hands of your enemies and destroyers; and moreover I should say that you were betraying your children; for you might bring them up and educate them; instead of which you go away and leave them and they will have to take their chance; . . .I beseech you therefore Socrates, to be persuaded by me, and to do as I say.*

Socrates: *Dear Crito, . . .I cannot put away the reasons which I have before given: The principles which I have hitherto honored and revered I still honor, and unless we can find other and better principles on the instant, I am certain not to agree with you; no, not even if the power of the multitude could inflict many more imprisonments, confiscations, deaths, frightening us like children with hobgoblin terrors.*
   —Plato, *Dialogues*

Sadeq Khalkháli (Islamic Judge): *So you are a Bahá'í.*

Bahar Vujdáni (Witness): *Yes.*

Judge: *Then you must convert immediately to the true faith of Islam; otherwise you will have to pay the sum of 500,000 tumans [approx. $80,000].*

Witness: *No.*

Judge: *What do you mean, no?*

Witness: *I cannot pay this sum. Even if I sold my shop and my home, I could not possibly realize 500,000 tumans.*

Judge: *In that case you will simply deny your ungodly beliefs, and you will be discharged.*

Witness: *No.*

Judge: *You will not say no this time. Your life depends on it. Think the matter over carefully.*

Witness: *I do not have the money you want from me and if I recanted, I would be a liar before God. You surely cannot force me to do this.*

Judge: *There is no God but God and Muhammad is His prophet. Make up your mind quickly.*

Witness: *No, I cannot deny my faith.*

Judge: *May God forgive you. I sentence you to death.*

The witness was taken out and shot.
—Reported by Marc Kravetz, *Irano Nox*

The two foregoing conversations both portray historical events. One occurs in a prison of ancient Greece, with Socrates as its main figure; the other takes place in a contemporary Islamic court in Iran, with a member of the Iranian Bahá'í community as the victim. In both cases the issue at hand is the struggle to reaffirm the fundamental nobility, integrity, and spirituality of human essence, and in both cases the choice open to the victims is denial of their own reality or death. Both choose to die rather than to deny or compromise their own reality. These two examples, dramatic as they are, are not rare.

The history of humanity is, in one sense, that of victory of the human spirit over all else. It is the history of the rise of knowledge, the expression of love, and the creation of civilization. It is the history of sciences, arts, and deeds of enlightenment, creativity, and care. This

102

history, however, was written in past ages by a few very remarkable individuals. Consequently, the history of humanity thus far is the story of the lives of a few historic figures. But with the coming of humanity's age of maturity, the history of the world will be written about the individuals, communities of people, and masses of humanity who will affect the course of history in a totally unique manner. Thus, in the study of issues related to peace, we need to focus on groups of people. For the purpose of this presentation on new approaches to violence, I have chosen the Bahá'í community for review and study because it is a contemporary, heterogeneous world community, with a well-documented history. Above all, the Bahá'í Faith is totally nonviolent and has been so from its very beginnings. All these characteristics render the Bahá'í community a befitting object of our search for new ways to conquer human violence. In order to appreciate fully the experience of the Bahá'í community in respect to its position regarding violence, it may be helpful to review briefly its history.

The Bahá'í era began in 1844 when a young man in Persia with the title of the Báb [The Gate] claimed fulfillment of the Islamic prophecies for the coming of the Promised One and inaugurated a religion of his own, the Bábí Faith. This new religion called upon its members to prepare themselves for the emergence of a new era in the history of mankind, an era in which humanity would at last be able to put aside its many differences and establish a lasting and universal peace. The Báb's teachings also changed many of the secondary laws of Islam. His claim created a considerable degree of fear and anger in the society as a whole and among the Islamic clergy in particular. The response of Muslims to the new religion was both fierce and predictable. They could not accept the advent of a new religion after Islam and collectively rose against the Bábí Faith with all their might and vehemence. Consequently, in a short span of nineteen years, thousands of Bábís were killed by government soldiers and ordinary citizens by the explicit decrees of Islamic religious leaders. The response of the Bábís to these persecutions was basically that of passive acceptance. However, in a few episodes, the Bábís resorted to self-defence, resulting in the deaths of about 2,000 Bábís. The fact that they resorted to defensive warfare created both a deep fear and a credible excuse for the Muslim clergy to sanction the killing of some 20,000 in total, all of whom were peaceful and defenceless men and women, both old and young. Major Eastern and Western historians attest the killings were cruel and barbaric in the extreme, and the violence inflicted on the Bábís was totally out of proportion with the

103

potential danger, if any, that they posed either to the government or the established religion, Islam. This response to the Bábís is better understood when we consider the fact that violence both begets and legitimizes violence, and consequently the limited defensive violence by the Bábís, at one level, was seen to justify the horrendous acts of violence perpetrated against them.

Violence creates fear which, in turn, calls for higher levels of violence. Under ordinary circumstances this process leads to a vicious cycle of violence, fear, more violence, and more fear. This condition is highly descriptive of the current politics of deterrence, which justify ever higher levels of armamentation and militarization of the planet and dangers of unimaginable violence. The case of the Bábís was different in the sense that the followers of the Báb did not respond to the fear and violence aimed at them with further violence, and after a few short years they abandoned their acts of self-defence altogether. This transformation was related to the main body of the teachings of the Báb. The Báb, on countless occasions, both in writing and during his verbal communication with his followers, stated that the primary purpose of his dispensation was to prepare his followers for the advent of Bahá'u'lláh [the Glory of God] who, the Báb informed them, would soon announce his mission to unify humanity and establish world peace. It was this promise of unity and peace which, in spite of enormous dangers, attracted thousands of the Iranian people to the Báb's religion and created a spiritual and social fervour of unparalleled intensity in Iran and its neighbouring countries. In this process many educated people, religious leaders, individuals with power and riches—both men and women—as well as thousands of ordinary people, such as peasants, farmers, shop-keepers and tradesmen, responded by becoming Bábís. Theirs was an affirmation of the remarkable power of the forces of unity and peace which attract people even under conditions of imminent danger. These multitudes accepted the new faith and began their active search for the advent of yet another new religion—the religion of unity and peace prophesied by the Báb.

In 1863, Bahá'u'lláh proclaimed his mission, and soon most of the Bábís and many others, primarily from Iran, countries under the rule of the Ottoman Empire, India, and southern regions of Russia, accepted the new faith and became known as Bahá'ís. This new faith had many remarkable characteristics and introduced the concept that humanity as a whole is in its adolescence, approaching its age of maturity. Bahá'u'lláh outlined some of the main characteristics of a mature human society, to be based, above all, on unity and the principle of the oneness of mankind, with men and women truly equal; science and religion in complete harmony; and society structured on the foundations of justice, universality, and absolute respect for the integrity and nobility of every individual. In a mature society, Bahá'u'lláh stated, universal education is essential, and intermediaries between man and God, such as the clergy, are unnecessary. Furthermore, in a mature and spiritualized human society there is no place for violence, and therefore violence of any kind is totally rejected in the Bahá'í Faith. Bahá'u'lláh admonished his followers to be agents of the unity of mankind; to avoid violence, anarchy, and war at all costs; and to refrain from participation in all destructive activities, including disunifying partisan politics. The majority of the early followers of Bahá'u'lláh were Bábís, and consequently Bahá'u'lláh's teachings had their immediate and most noticeable effect on these individuals. Bahá'u'lláh Himself comments on the transformation of the Bábí community as a direct result of responding to his councils by adopting this new approach to violence:

> It was through the grace of God and with the aid of seemly words
> and praiseworthy deeds that the unsheathed swords of the Bábí
> community were returned to their scabbards. Indeed through
> the power of good words, the righteous have always succeeded
> in winning command over the meads of the hearts of men.[1]

Bahá'u'lláh, later in the same statement, elaborates upon the characteristics of this new approach to violence and describes the remarkable powers of love which can be harnessed by "good words" and "righteous deeds." These qualities are at the core of human behaviour in a new world order which will be fuelled by the forces of love and unity. In this new world, human violence and disunity are not elevated to the levels of legitimate and inherent qualities of human nature and civilization; rather, they are viewed as the absence of the forces of love and unity. Such a perspective demands that we focus most of our attention and resources on those activities and practices which will promote love and unity, and not on those which attempt to counter and neutralize the effects of violence and disunity. The Bahá'í approach to human violence, therefore, is to prevent its occurrence by promoting higher levels of love and unity and, at the same time, strengthening the foundations of justice so the perpetrators of violence will not be encouraged in their lifestyle because of laxity in the application of the principles of justice. Such an approach requires transformation both in the individual and institutional life of humanity. In the same

Tablet* by Bahá'u'lláh referred to above, there are a number of guidelines for individual and collective behaviour conducive to this new approach to violence:

> Thy day of service is now come. . . .Thou must show forth that which will ensure the peace and the well-being of the miserable and the downtrodden. Gird up the loins of thine endeavour, that perchance thou mayest release the captive from his chains, and enable him to attain unto true liberty. . . .Strife and conflict befit the beasts of the wild. . . .beware lest your hands or tongues cause harm to anyone among mankind. . . .Arise, O people, and, by the power of God's might, resolve to gain the victory over your own selves. . . .Do not busy yourselves in your own concerns; let your thoughts be fixed upon that which will rehabilitate the fortunes of mankind and sanctify the hearts and souls of men. This can best be achieved through pure and holy deeds, through a virtuous life and a goodly behaviour. . . .Let your vision be world-embracing, rather than confined to your own self. . . .It is incumbent upon every man, in this Day, to hold fast unto whatsoever will promote the interests, and exalt the station of all nations and just governments. . . .Consort with the followers of all religions in a spirit of friendliness and fellowship. . . .It is not his to boast who loveth his country, but it is his who loveth the world. . . .O people of Justice! Be as brilliant as the light and as splendid as the fire. . . .The brightness of the fire of your love will no doubt fuse and unify the contending peoples and kindreds of the earth, whilst the fierceness of the flame of enmity and hatred cannot but result in strife and ruin. . . .The distinguishing feature that marketh the pre-eminent character of this Supreme Revelation consisteth in that We have, on the one hand, blotted out from the pages of God's holy Book whatsoever hath been the cause of strife, of malice and mischief amongst the children of men, and have, on the other, laid down the essential prerequisites of concord, of understanding, of complete and enduring unity. . . .Time and

---

*Bahá'u'lláh, during his lifetime, wrote many books, a large number of shorter works referred to as "Tablets," and innumerable letters to various individuals. All these works, together with the writings of the Báb and 'Abdu'l-Bahá, constitute the holy scriptures of the Bahá'í Faith.

again have We admonished Our beloved ones to avoid, nay to flee from, anything whatsoever from which the odour of mischief can be detected. . . .Let them that bear allegiance to this Wronged One [Bahá'u'lláh] be even as a raining cloud in moments of charity and benevolence and as a blazing fire in restraining their base and appetitive natures.[2]

This new perspective on the purpose of life and approach to human violence, characterized by the life-giving and constructive acts of love, care, kindness, and celebration of all that is positive, creative, and unifying, is further elaborated upon by 'Abdu'l-Bahá in the following manner:

Act in accordance with the counsels of the Lord: that is, rise up in such wise, and with such qualities, as to endow the body of this world with a living soul, and to bring this young child, humanity, to the stage of adulthood. So far as ye are able, ignite a candle of love in every meeting, and with tenderness rejoice and cheer ye every heart. Care for the stranger as for one of your own; show to alien souls the same loving kindness ye bestow upon your faithful friends. Should any come to blows with you, seek to be friends with him; should any stab you to the heart, be ye a healing salve unto his sores; should any taunt and mock at you, meet him with love. Should any heap his blame upon you, praise ye him; should he offer you a deadly poison, give him the choicest honey in exchange; and should he threaten your life, grant him a remedy that will heal him evermore. Should he be pain itself, be ye his medicine; should he be thorns, be ye his roses and sweet herbs. Perchance such ways and words from you will make this darksome world turn bright at last; will make this dusty earth turn heavenly, this devilish prison place become a royal palace of the Lord—so that war and strife will pass and be no more, and love and trust will pitch their tents on the summits of the world. Such is the essence of God's admonitions; such in sum are the teachings for the Dispensation of Bahá [Bahá'u'lláh].[3]

The response of the Bahá'ís to these guidelines was complete and absolute. Consequently, they introduced a new way of dealing with the violence perpetrated against them by the Muslim clergy, government soldiers, and the ordinary but fanatical citizens of Iran. A campaign, as fierce and vehement as those waged against the Bábís, was initiated against the Bahá'ís. Arrests, torture, and killings began throughout Iran, and there was fear that the newly-established faith would be totally destroyed. However, it survived the onslaught, flourished, spread to many parts of the world, and established in a span of about one century a worldwide community. Its several million adherents are scattered all over the globe and represent many of the nations, races, religions, and languages of the world. The Bahá'í Faith is now well on its way to providing the prototype of a new world order.

There are a number of reasons for the growth of the Bahá'í community, and one of the most important is the manner in which the Bahá'ís have responded to violence aimed against them. They have countered violence with love and at every opportunity have pointed out to their aggressors and opponents the reality of the unity of mankind and the essential nobility and spirituality of every human being. On countless occasions and as a response to the many atrocities inflicted upon them, the Bahá'ís have reiterated their belief in the necessity of safeguarding the nobility and integrity of human reality, and to this end, they have dedicated all their efforts, individually and as a community, towards the establishment of a united, spiritually-oriented community. In this process the Bahá'ís have developed a new mind-set about human nature and a new paradigm for dealing with human violence, both of which can be summarized in the concept "unity in diversity."[4]

When the world and its people are viewed from the perspective of unity, it becomes not only counterproductive, but also impossible to respond to violence with violence, disregard, passivity, or rationalizations. The most effective and essential response is obviously that which would counter the destructive forces of violence with a more powerful and constructive force, and this is only possible when the individual and the community commit all their resources to the promotion of acts of love, justice, equality, and unity. Such a lifestyle will ultimately create peace. During the past few years in Iran, the Bahá'í community, while subject to considerable brutality and violence, has responded with acts of love and unity and with continuous demands for justice and equality.[5]

The Islamic Revolutionary government of Iran, from the very first days of its existence in 1979, began an all-out campaign of violence against the Bahá'ís of Iran. Soon all members of the Bahá'í community, some 300,000 in number, became outcasts in their own country. Under the Islamic constitution (as in the previous constitution) Bahá'ís, unlike all other religious minorities, were given no civil rights, no rights to own property, to marry according to the Bahá'í laws, to secure employment, or to be counted as citizens of their homeland. The Bahá'ís, both individually and through their administrative institutions, responded with courage, reason, and appeals for justice on the one hand and with acts of civil obedience, cooperation, love, and humanity on the other. Under conditions of injustice, imprisonment, brutality, and murder, and while enduring profound acts of inhumanity, they remained the most outspoken defendants of the fundamental nobility of humankind. The Bahá'ís of Iran have emerged victorious, as a united, optimistic, courageous, and loving community of people who continue to counter violence and tyranny aimed at them with love and the pursuit of justice. They have become known to the world as a peace-loving community of people who will neither respond to violence with violence, nor accept it without countering violence with love and continuing to demand justice.

Because of these actions, the Bahá'ís of Iran have gained both the sympathy and respect of the enlightened peoples and governments of the world and so offer a unique example of the transcendence of violence through harnessing the "energies of love." The Bahá'ís of Iran and their coreligionists around the world form a "global community" which merits study as a prototype for a peaceful world, so clearly needed at this point in the collective growth of humanity. The next chapter will briefly outline the characteristics of the new world envisioned by Bahá'u'lláh.

11

The Emerging New World Order

Soon will the present-day order be rolled up, and a new one spread out in its stead.
—Bahá'u'lláh

We begin to perceive that the mode of being of a national state is incompatible with the reality of the modern age with its overarching problems. But we have not been able to put forward a suggestion to change it.
—Aurelio Peccei

Harnessing the forces of love to nullify the forces of violence and war requires not only a fundamental change in the mind-set and behaviour of individual human beings, but also a restructuring of human society so that it can function as an appropriate channel for the forces of love such as unity, equality, freedom, justice, cooperation, tenderness, care, and creativity, which are released through people's actions.

As they now exist, the social and political organizations of the world are appropriate, at best, to deal with disunity, bondage, injustice, corruption, harshness, indifference, and destruction; at their worst, they cause these negative conditions. But these are characteristics of a dying order, the by-products of the ignorant age of our collective childhood and the rebellious era of our adolescence. With the advent of mankind's age of maturity, a new world order must take the place of the old—a new order able to channel and use the enormous creative energies which are released as people begin to learn to harness the forces of love. This new order must be congruent with the needs of a rapidly-evolving humanity and allow for the creation and progress of an ever-advancing civilization characterized by unity and harmony at all levels—among people, between science and religion, and in the continuum of past, present, and future.

At the end of his book, *The Tao of Physics*, while commenting on new discoveries in physics, Fritjof Capra writes:

> I believe that the world-view implied by modern physics is inconsistent with our present society, which does not reflect the harmonious interrelatedness we observe in nature. To achieve such a state of dynamic balance, a radically different social and economic structure will be needed: a cultural revolution in the true sense of the word. The survival of our whole civilization may depend on whether we can bring about such a change.[1]

The "cultural revolution in the true sense of the word" of which Capra speaks cannot be anything but a spiritual revolution, in which mankind is finally freed from its animal heritage and embarks on an unparalleled period in its history of collective evolution. During this period, spiritual qualities of knowledge, love, and service will dominate all human affairs, and creativity and justice will be among the rights and opportunities which people will enjoy, with cooperation and the pursuit of excellence making possible the fulfillment of humanity's highest and oldest aspirations. The transformation of human society into a global society governed by the laws of a new world order is not only desirable but also, in fact, inevitable.

This period of evolution is the coming of age of mankind, the transition of humanity from childhood to adulthood. John Naisbitt, in his book, *Megatrends*, refers to the "time of parenthesis," by which he means a period of transition from one era in human history to another. According to Naisbitt, the major transitions of our time are from the industrial to the information society, from forced technology to high tech and high touch technology, from national to world economy, from short-term to long-term objectives, from centralization to decentralization, from institutional help to self-help, from representative to participatory democracy, from hierarchies to networking, from the dominance of the North to equal participation of the so-called South nations, and from either/or to multiple options.[2]

I have listed the table of contents of Naisbitt's book in order to illustrate that all the changes which he identifies are, in fact, changes characteristic of a world moving through childhood and adolescence to adulthood. He is, of course, not alone in his observations; many individuals and groups of people, in fact, have commented on this change. Ervin Laszlo speaks of the emergence of a world Solidarity Revolution. He says:

> A new world order will come about when the people of all nations demand of their leaders that they be given a constructive role in building the shared human future; when a new global ethos emerges based on trust and solidarity; when a new standard of humanism crystallizes as the norm of conduct in all major areas of public policy.[3]

Here Laszlo is speaking about maturity and unity, the two main themes of this book. People will be able to play a constructive role in building a new world order once they have attained a level of maturity and responsibility. The emergence of a "new global ethos based on trust and solidarity," likewise, depends on the ability of humanity to unite, a quality of the age of maturity.

Alvin Toffler looks at this period in human history from the perspective of change, which sets our time apart from the past in a most dramatic way. He observes:

> Indeed, a growing body of reputable opinion asserts that the present movement represents nothing less than the second great divide in human history, comparable in magnitude only with that first great break in historic continuity, the shift from barbarism to civilization.[4]

The shift from barbarism to civilization was the most remarkable achievement of mankind in relation to unity, and a similar shift must now take place, from a civilization focussed on materialism and individualism to one that is spiritual and universal. The characterizations of this process as the advent of a "cultural revolution in the true sense of the word" (Capra), transition from "the age of parenthesis" (Naisbitt), or the emergence of "world solidarity" (Laszlo), or "the second great divide" (Toffler) are different expressions of our collective progression toward the creation of a new world order.

The early glimmerings of such an order are already apparent everywhere, and some of its cardinal characteristics are described by Shoghi Effendi. He says:

> Far from aiming at the subversion of the existing foundations of society, it seeks to broaden its basis, to remold its institutions in a manner consonant with the needs of an ever-changing world. It can conflict with no legitimate allegiances nor can it undermine essential loyalties. Its purpose is neither to stifle the flame of a sane and intelligent patriotism in men's hearts nor to abolish the system of national autonomy so essential if the evils of excessive centralization are to be avoided. It does not ignore, nor does it attempt to suppress, the diversity of ethnical origins, of climate, of history, of language and tradition, of thought and habit, that differentiate the peoples and nations of the world. It calls for a wider loyalty, for a larger aspiration than any that has animated the human race. It insists upon the subordination of national impulses and interests to the imperative claims of a unified world. It repudiates excessive centralization on one hand, and disclaims all attempts at uniformity on the other. Its watchword is unity in diversity. . . .[5]

Shoghi Effendi, to whom this book is dedicated, provides us with a most exciting description of the future human society, and I wish to quote extensively from one of his statements about the characteristics of the emerging new world order:

> A mechanism of world inter-communication will be devised, embracing the whole planet, freed from national hindrances and restrictions, and functioning with marvelous swiftness and perfect regularity. A world metropolis will act as the nerve center of a world civilization, the focus towards which the unifying forces of life will converge and from which its energizing influences will radiate. A world language will either be invented or chosen from among the existing languages and will be taught in the schools of all the federated nations as an auxiliary to their mother tongue. A world script, a world literature, a uniform and universal system of currency, of weights and measures, will simplify and facilitate intercourse and understanding among the

nations and races of mankind. In such a world society, science and religion, the two most potent forces in human life, will be reconciled, will coöperate, and will harmoniously develop. The press will, under such a system, while giving full scope to the expression of the diversified views and convictions of mankind, cease to be mischievously manipulated by vested interests, whether private or public, and will be liberated from the influence of contending governments and peoples. The economic resources of the world will be organized, its sources of raw materials will be tapped and fully utilized, its markets will be coördinated and developed, and the distribution of its products will be equitably regulated.

National rivalries, hatreds, and intrigues will cease, and racial animosity and prejudice will be replaced by racial amity, understanding and coöperation. The causes of religious strife will be permanently removed, economic barriers and restrictions will be completely abolished, and the inordinate distinction between classes will be obliterated. Destitution on the one hand, and gross accumulation of ownership on the other, will disappear. The enormous energy dissipated and wasted on war, whether economic or political, will be consecrated to such ends as will extend the range of human inventions and technical development, to the increase of the productivity of mankind, to the extermination of disease, to the extension of scientific research, to the raising of the standard of physical health, to the sharpening and refinement of the human brain, to the exploitation of the unused and unsuspected resources of the planet, to the prolongation of human life, and to the furtherance of any other agency that can stimulate the intellectual, the moral, and spiritual life of the entire human race.[6]

While a detailed description and analysis of the characteristics of this emerging new world order are beyond the scope of this book, this discussion would be incomplete if two of its major characteristics were not at least briefly discussed. These are the processes of conflict resolution and the politics of transformation. Our current practices in respect to conflict resolution are, generally speaking, neither greatly successful in the development of higher levels of harmony and cooperation among differing peoples, ideologies, and interests, nor are the prevalent perspectives on the

115

politics of transformation in accord with the concept of the unity paradigm, which demands the safeguard of the creative diversity of peoples and cultures within the framework of a united world community. Unless new approaches to conflict resolution are put into motion and new perspectives on the transformation of human societies are offered, our attempts to create a new world order within the parameters of the unity paradigm will be futile.

Bahá'í Consultation: Conflict Resolution within the Unity Paradigm

They must make the cause of peace the object of general consultation. . . . .
　　—'Abdu'l-Bahá

The ordinary use of the words "consultation" and "consulting" refers to the processes of deliberation, advice-seeking, and information-gathering from various sources, especially from professional experts such as physicians, engineers, lawyers, and others. The Bahá'í concept of consultation, however, is unique and, at least in part, describes that human endeavour in which a small or large number of individuals, representing themselves, institutions, nations, or any other group of people, communicate with one another in an atmosphere of complete unity and frankness. Their purpose is to seek out the truth about the object of their deliberation and to find ways and means in which individual and societal needs for justice, equality, freedom, and progress are met. They also deliberate on ways human conflicts can be resolved without the abuse of power or the manipulation or denial and violation of human rights of any people, whether or not they are directly involved in these consultative processes.

　　This type of consultation requires high levels of emotional and intellectual maturity and high spiritual, moral, and ethical standards from its participants. Therefore, Bahá'í consultation is most effective within a framework characterized by growth-orientation, unity in diversity, creativity, and cooperation. These are features of an integrated and comprehensive approach to human endeavours which are totally incompatible with the authoritarian and indulgent modes of human relationships. The

116

main objective of Bahá'í consultation, therefore, is to bring about circumstances in which the seemingly contradictory principles of "mercy and justice, of freedom and submission, of the sanctity of the right of the individual and of self-surrender, of vigilance, discretion, and prudence on the one hand, and fellowship, candour, and courage on the other," are reconciled and human conflicts are resolved in a creative manner with the constant goal of searching out truth and not becoming prey to the forces of prejudice, ignorance, self-interest, or mistrust.[7]

The principal prerequisite for the achievement of these objectives is unity. "The first condition" of consultation, 'Abdu'l-Bahá affirms, "is absolute love and harmony amongst the members of the Assembly [the consultative body]. They must be wholly free from estrangement. . . .Should harmony of thought and absolute unity be non-existent, that gathering shall be dispersed and that Assembly be brought to naught."[8]

The most important quality which the participants in consultation should continually endeavour to attain is a condition of maturity and spirituality. From the Bahá'í perspective, maturity and spirituality are the same, and both denote the ability of the individual to be prayerful, humble, patient, courteous, dignified, caring, and moderate. In the words of 'Abdu'l-Bahá, "They must in every matter search out the truth and not insist upon their own opinion, for stubbornness and persistence in one's views will lead ultimately to discord and wrangling and the truth will remain hidden."[9]

The secret of unity and maturity called for in Bahá'í consultation lies in the ability of the participants to express themselves "with absolute freedom" in putting forth their arguments. Should anyone oppose, they "must on no account feel hurt for not until matters are fully discussed can the right way be revealed. The shining spark of truth cometh forth only after the clash of differing opinions. If, after discussion a decision be carried unanimously, well and good; but if. . . difference of opinion should arise, a majority of voices must prevail. . . ."[10]

Within this framework, the focus of Bahá'í consultation will be on those issues which result in higher standards and universal availability of education, health, and economic well-being; which bring about the eradication of the extremes of wealth and poverty; which encourage ever higher levels of love, care, and kindness among people; and which foster the creation of conditions of equality, justice, freedom and a peaceful, orderly, and harmonious individual and social life.

This method of consultation is an excellent tool for the attainment of some of the major objectives of the new world order based on the principles of the unity paradigm.

Politics of Transformation

. . .is not the object of every Revelation to effect a transformation in the whole character of mankind, a transformation that shall manifest itself both outwardly and inwardly, that shall affect both its inner life and external conditions? For if the character of mankind be not changed, the futility of God's universal Manifestations would be apparent.
—Bahá'u'lláh

Human societies are transformed through a multitude of causes which, on the surface, seem to be unrelated or only partially related. These causes may be economic, social, or political in nature, may come about as a result of revolutions, technological and scientific innovations, ideological and conceptual developments, or organizational and structural changes introduced into an already established but increasingly inadequate order. While these and similar approaches to the transformation of human societies have been and continue to be used to bring about change in conformity with certain individual and group perspectives and ideologies, in the final analysis all successful transformation of human societies must, of necessity, conform to universal laws of growth.

These laws, as discussed previously, propel humanity forward and help it gradually but definitely move through stages of infancy, childhood, and adolescence to those of adulthood and maturity. Ultimately, a mature society will be characterized by unity in diversity, the harmony of science and religion, the equality of men and women, and by the eradication of prejudices of all kinds, the preservation of human rights, and the promotion of justice and freedom—in short, by the assertion of the fundamental nobility of every human being and the ultimate victory of the human spirit.

The Bahá'í perspective on this emerging new world order sees the necessity for the conscious development of a politics of transformation which will harness the inherent and inviolable laws of life and growth governing human societies. Such an approach to the introduction of societal change must be based on the principle of unity in diversity and must have as its ultimate goal the establishment of global peace. Growth dynamics of human societies, like those of individual human beings, are both natural and intentional. They are natural in the sense that the organism, in this case the society, either continues to grow and evolve, or becomes rigid and begins its gradual or rapid process of disintegration, decay, and destruction. These growth dynamics are also intentional, in the sense that although all societies are subject to these universal laws of growth, the nature of their individual growth is unique to each. Human beings and human societies are creative entities, and in the process of their growth they introduce those unique dimensions that make our world diverse, united, and beautiful.

The new world order must be able to accommodate all these dynamics and processes so that the politics of transformation will become the same as the politics of enlightened maturation, assuring the advent of a new world order, the order of peace.

Epilogue

Peace is the fruit of the tree of human unity, and unity is the hallmark of humanity's coming of age. Humanity, in its long march toward maturity, has struggled to free itself from the evils of self-centredness, aggression, injustice, tyranny, prejudice, and ignorance. The universal human yearning for love, peace, beauty, and knowledge has its source in human spiritual nature. The coming of age of mankind is, above all, the era of the spiritualization of the life and world of humanity. True maturity can at last flourish, a new way of behaviour and a new outlook about life can develop, and a new world order can be established. Attempts to create equality of the sexes, the harmony of science and religion, cooperation and mutual trust between warring nations, races, and religions, and finally the oneness of humanity are all spiritual undertakings that will ultimately lead to the creation of a united global society.

The citizens of this united world will be engaged in the creation of a technology of peace, the organization of a cooperative and just society, and the elimination of the causes of prejudice and discord. In dealing with violence, a united world will depend on the constructive and life-engendering forces of love, growth, cooperation, and unity, rather than outdated practices based on hatred, rigidity, competition, and war. But, above all, the united people of this new world will end the age of humanity's captivity in the bondage of its animal heritage, ignorance, and materialism, and they will usher in the era of enlightenment, spirituality, and an ever-advancing civilization. Then will the spiritually-enlightened and highly creative people of the united world harness the forces of love and usher in the era of the "Most Great Peace."

Notes

Chapter 1. THE ETERNAL QUEST FOR PEACE: AN INTRODUCTION

1. Natalya Reshetovskaya, *Sanya: My Husband Aleksandr Solzhenitsyn,* trans. Elena Ivanoff (London: Hart-Davis, MacGibbon, 1975), p. 31.

2. Dee Brown, *Bury My Heart at Wounded Knee: An Indian History of the American West* (New York: Holt, Rinehart and Winston, 1970), p. 439.

3. Leo Tolstoy, *War and Peace,* trans. Constance Garnett (New York: The Modern Library, 1931), p. 611.

4. Bahá'u'lláh, cited in *The Promised Day is Come,* Shoghi Effendi, 3d ed. (Wilmette, Illinois: Bahá'í Publishing Trust, 1980), p. 116.

5. Aurelio Peccei and Alexander King, Foreword to *Goals for Mankind: A Report to the Club of Rome on the New Horizons of Global Community,* ed. Ervin Laszlo et al. (New York: E.P. Dutton, 1977), p. vii.

Chapter 2. A LOOK AT THE PRESENT: FROM SEPARATION TO UNITY

1. Janez Stanovnik, "The Debit Balance of the Mistakes of Several Decades," in *What Kind of a World Are We Leaving Our Children?* (Paris: UNESCO, 1978), p. 73.

2. 'Abdu'l-Bahá, *Selections from the Writings of 'Abdu'l-Bahá,* trans. Marzieh Gail et al. (Haifa: Bahá'í World Centre, 1978), p. 284.

3. Bahá'u'lláh, *Gleanings from the Writings of Bahá'u'lláh,* trans. Shoghi Effendi, 2d ed. (Wilmette, Illinois: Bahá'í Publishing Trust, 1976), p. 250.

4. Fritjof Capra, *The Turning Point: Science, Society, and the Rising Culture* (Toronto: Bantam Books, 1983), p. 224.

5. A general discussion of this topic can be found in *Family Violence: An International and Interdisciplinary Study,* ed. John M. Eekelaar and Sanford N. Katz (Toronto: Butterworth, 1978).

6. 'Abdu'l-Bahá, *Paris Talks: Addresses Given by 'Abdu'l-Bahá in Paris in 1911-1912,* 11th ed. (London: Bahá'í Publishing Trust, 1969), pp. 36-37.

7. See Sigmund Freud, "Why War?" in *Complete Psychological Works,* Standard Edition, trans. J. Strachey (London: Hogarth Press, 1964), pp. 197-213.

8. Konrad Lorenz, *On Aggression,* trans. Marjorie Latzke (London: Methuen and Co., 1966), p. 186.

9. Ashley Montagu, *Man and Aggression* (New York: Oxford University Press, 1968), p. 8.

10. Montagu, *Man and Aggression,* p. 6.

11. Richard E. Leakey and Roger Lewin, *Origins: What New Discoveries Reveal about the Emergence of Our Species and its Possible Future* (New York: E.P. Dutton, 1977), p. 10.

12. Leakey and Lewin, p. 10.

13. Hossain B. Danesh, "The Violence-Free Society: A Gift for Our Children," 2d ed., *Bahá'í Studies*, vol. 6 (October 1979), pp. 8-12.

14. These theories are discussed in "Defining and Studying Romantic Love," by Kenneth S. Pope in *On Love and Loving*, ed. Kenneth S. Pope et al. (San Francisco: Jossey-Bass Publishers, 1980), pp. 1-3.

15. Arno Plack, quoted in *The Imperishable Dominion*, Udo Schaefer, trans. Janet Rawling-Keitel, David Hopper and Patricia Crampton (Oxford: George Ronald, 1983), p. 46.

16. See *On Love and Loving*, pp. 3-4.

17. 'Abdu'l-Bahá, *Foundations of World Unity* (Wilmette, Illinois: Bahá'í Publishing Trust, 1971), pp. 88-89.

18. Arnold Toynbee, *A Study of History* (New York: Oxford University Press, 1972), p. 228.

19. These events are discussed extensively throughout *The Promised Day is Come* by Shoghi Effendi.

20. Shoghi Effendi, *World Order of Bahá'u'lláh, Selected Letters*, 2d ed. (Wilmette, Illinois: Bahá'í Publishing Trust, 1974), p. 42.

21. Aurelio Peccei, "The Imperative of a New Humanism," in *Dilemmas of Modern Man* (Winnipeg, Canada: Great-West Life Assurance Company, 1975), p. 21.

22. Capra, p. 278.

23. Ervin Laszlo, quoted in *The Turning Point*, p. 288.

Chapter 3. ON THE NATURE OF PEACE AND HAPPINESS

1. Roderic Gorney, *The Human Agenda* (New York: Bantam Books, 1973), p. 490.

2. Albert Einstein, quoted in *The Human Agenda*, p. 490.

3. 'Abdu'l-Bahá, *Selections*, p. 286.

4. 'Abdu'l-Bahá, *The Secret of Divine Civilization*, trans. Marzieh Gail, 3d ed. (Wilmette, Illinois: Bahá'í Publishing Trust, 1975), pp. 23-24.

5. Bahá'u'lláh, *The Seven Valleys and the Four Valleys*, trans. Marzieh Gail, 3d ed. (Wilmette, Illinois: Bahá'í Publishing Trust, 1978), pp. 17-18.

6. George Bernard Shaw, "The Revolutionist's Handbook and Pocket Companion" in the Ayot St. Lawrence Edition of *The Collected Works of Bernard Shaw*, vol. 10, *Man and Superman* (New York: Wm. H. Wise, 1930), p. 224.

7. Bahá'u'lláh, *Gleanings*, p. 286.

8. Bahá'u'lláh, *Gleanings*, p. 217.

Chapter 4. DEVELOPING A NEW MIND-SET

1. Capra, p. 266.

2. Capra, p. 47.

3. Leakey and Lewin, p. 256.

4. Peccei and King, p. xi.

5. Bahá'u'lláh, *Gleanings*, pp. 254-55.

6. 'Abdu'l-Bahá, *Selections*, p. 297.

7. Shoghi Effendi, *The Promised Day is Come*, pp. 113-14.

8. Shoghi Effendi, *World Order of Bahá'u'lláh*, p. 202.

9. Shoghi Effendi, *World Order of Bahá'u'lláh*, p. 43.

10. Bahá'u'lláh, *Gleanings*, p. 213.

11. H.M. Balyuzi, *'Abdu'l-Bahá* (Oxford: George Ronald, 1971), p. 258.

12. Shoghi Effendi, *The Advent of Divine Justice*, 3d ed. (Wilmette, Illinois: Bahá'í Publishing Trust, 1969), p. 74.

13. Universal House of Justice, *Messages from the Universal House of Justice, 1968-1973* (Wilmette, Illinois: Bahá'í Publishing Trust, 1976), pp. 33-34.

14. Universal House of Justice, *Messages,* pp. 33-34.

15. 'Abdu'l-Bahá, *The Promulgation of Universal Peace*, comp. Howard MacNutt, 2d ed. (Wilmette, Illinois: Bahá'í Publishing Trust, 1982), p. 175.

16. 'Abdu'l-Bahá, *Promulgation*, pp. 174-75.

17. *Webster's New World Dictionary*, college ed., s.v. "equal."

18. 'Abdu'l-Bahá, *Selections*, p. 302.

19. 'Abdu'l-Bahá, *Paris Talks*, p. 133.

20. 'Abdu'l-Bahá, *Bahá'í World Faith: Selected Writings of Bahá'u'lláh and 'Abdu'l-Bahá*, rev. ed. (Wilmette, Illinois: Bahá'í Publishing Trust, 1956), p. 241.

21. 'Abdu'l-Bahá, *Star of the West*, vol. 3, no. 3 (Chicago: Bahá'í News Service, April 28, 1912), p. 4.

Chapter 5. Uses and Abuses of Power and Love in Human Relationships

1. This concept has been developed by T.W. Adorno in *The Authoritarian Personality* (New York: Harper, 1950).

2. Erich Fromm, *Escape from Freedom* (New York: Avon Books, 1969), pp. 190-91.

3. Rollo May, *Power and Innocence: A Search for the Sources of Violence* (New York: Delta Books, 1972), pp. 105-13.

4. This concept is discussed at length in "Prejudice: Is It Societal or Personal?" in *The Person in Psychology: Selected Essays*, Gordon W. Allport (Boston: Beacon Press, 1968), pp. 195-99.

5. Christopher Lasch, *The Culture of Narcissism* (New York: W.W. Norton, 1978), p. 4.

6. The concepts outlined in the following pages are contained in the author's work in progress, tentatively entitled, *The Integrated Self.*

Chapter 6. The Challenge of Freedom

1. Freud's ideas are discussed by Bruno Bettelheim in "The Ultimate Limit," in *Surviving and Other Essays* (New York: Vintage Books, 1980), p. 9.

2. Bettelheim, p. 9.

3. Bettelheim, p. 9.
4. Bettelheim, p. 10.
5. Fromm, *Escape from Freedom*, p. 40.
6. Fromm, *Escape From Freedom*, p. 39.
7. Leakey and Lewin, p. 8.
8. 'Abdu'l-Bahá, *Selections*, p. 302.
9. 'Abdu'l-Bahá, *Selections*, p. 302.
10. 'Abdu'l-Bahá, *Paris Talks*, pp. 41-42.
11. Bahá'u'lláh, *Gleanings*, pp. 215-16.
12. Bahá'u'lláh, *A Synopsis and Codification of the Laws and Ordinances of the Kitáb-i-Aqdas*, comp. The Universal House of Justice (Haifa: Bahá'í World Centre, 1973), p. 25.
13. Peccei, p. 21.
14. Bahá'u'lláh, *Tablets of Bahá'u'lláh, Revealed after the Kitáb-i-Aqdas* (Haifa: Bahá'í World Centre, 1978), pp. 66-68.

Chapter 7. CREATING A TECHNOLOGY OF PEACE

1. Adlai Stevenson, from a speech given in Hartford, Connecticut, Sept. 18, 1952.
2. Floyd Matson, *The Idea of Man* (New York: Delacorte Press, 1976), pp. 11-12.
3. 'Abdu'l-Bahá, *Paris Talks*, p. 97.
4. Allen Weelis, "Spirit," in *The Mind's I*, ed. Douglas R. Hofstadter and Daniel C. Dennett (Toronto: Bantam Books, 1982), p. 119.
5. 'Abdu'l-Bahá, *Some Answered Questions*, trans. Laura Clifford Barney, 3d ed. (Wilmette, Illinois: Bahá'í Publishing Trust, 1981), p. 200.
6. 'Abdu'l-Bahá, *Some Answered Questions*, p. 201.
7. Stanovnik, p. 73.
8. Stanovnik, p. 74.
9. 'Abdu'l-Bahá, *Paris Talks*, p. 97.
10. Peccei, p. 19.
11. Frederick Turner, "Escape From Modernism," *Harper's* (Nov. 1984), p. 49.
12. Turner, p. 50.
13. Turner, p. 50.
14. Capra, p. 265.
15. 'Abdu'l-Bahá, *Paris Talks*, pp. 143-46.
16. Albert Einstein, *Out of My Later Years* (New York: Philosophical Library, 1950), p. 26.
17. Jacob Bronowski, *The Ascent of Man* (Boston: Little, Brown and Co., 1973), p. 256.
18. 'Abdu'l-Bahá, *Bahá'í World Faith*, pp. 224-25.

Chapter 8. PEACE AND THE NEW WORLD ORDER: REALITY OR UTOPIA?

1. 'Abdu'l-Bahá, *Bahá'í World Faith*, p. 257.

2. 'Abdu'l-Bahá, *Selections*, pp. 31-32.
3. 'Abdu'l-Bahá, *Selections*, p. 32.
4. Leakey and Lewin, p. 256.
5. Shoghi Effendi, *World Order of Bahá'u'lláh*, p. 43.

Chapter 9. A SYMPTOM NOT A DISEASE: A NEW PERSPECTIVE ON VIOLENCE

1. Lorenz, *On Aggression*, p. 238.
2. See Lorenz, *On Aggression*, pp. 245-46.
3. Richard B. Gregg, *The Power of Nonviolence*, 2d ed. (New York: Schocken Books, 1966), pp. 43-44.
4. Bertrand Russell, from *Justice in War Time*, quoted in Gregg, p. 70.
5. Gregg, p. 71.
6. Jean-Paul Sartre, *The Anti-Semite and Jew* (New York: Schocken Books, 1948), p. 53.

Chapter 10. VIOLENCE DISARMED: A CONTEMPORARY EXAMPLE

1. Bahá'u'lláh, *Tablets of Bahá'u'lláh*, p. 85.
2. Bahá'u'lláh, *Tablets of Bahá'u'lláh*, pp. 84-94.
3. 'Abdu'l-Bahá, *Selections*, p. 34.
4. For a detailed discussion of this concept, see 'Abdu'l-Bahá, *Selections*, pp. 291-92.
5. An account of the persecutions of the Iranian Bahá'í community, past and present, is documented in "The Persecution of the Bahá'ís of Iran 1844-1984," Douglas Martin, *Bahá'í Studies*, vol. 12/13 (1984).

Chapter 11. THE EMERGING NEW WORLD ORDER

1. Capra cites this passage in *The Turning Point*, p. 17.
2. These concepts have been developed by John Naisbitt in *Megatrends* (New York: Warner Books, 1984).
3. Laszlo, p. 366.
4. Alvin Toffler, *Future Shock* (New York: Bantam Books, 1971), p. 12.
5. Shoghi Effendi, *World Order of Bahá'u'lláh*, pp. 41-42.
6. Shoghi Effendi, *World Order of Bahá'u'lláh*, pp. 203-4.
7. Shoghi Effendi, *Principles of Bahá'í Administration*, 3d ed. (London: Bahá'í Publishing Trust, 1973), p. 44.
8. Shoghi Effendi, *Principles*, pp. 42-43.
9. Shoghi Effendi, *Principles*, p. 43.
10. Shoghi Effendi, *Principles*, p. 42.

Bibliography

'Abdu'l-Bahá. *Foundations of World Unity*. Wilmette, Illinois: Bahá'í Publishing Trust, 1971.

_____. *Paris Talks: Addresses Given by 'Abdu'l-Bahá in Paris in 1911-1912*. 11th ed. London: Bahá'í Publishing Trust, 1969.

_____. *The Promulgation of Universal Peace*. Comp. Howard MacNutt. 2d ed. Wilmette, Illinois: Bahá'í Publishing Trust, 1982.

_____. *The Secret of Divine Civilization*. Trans. Marzieh Gail. 3d ed. Wilmette, Illinois: Bahá'í Publishing Trust, 1975.

_____. *Selections from the Writings of 'Abdu'l-Bahá*. Trans. Marzieh Gail et al. Haifa: Bahá'í World Centre, 1978.

_____. *Some Answered Questions*. Trans. Laura Clifford Barney. 3d ed. Wilmette, Illinois: Bahá'í Publishing Trust, 1981.

_____. *Star of the West*. Vol. 3, no. 3. Chicago: Bahá'í News Service, April 28, 1912.

'Abdu'l-Bahá and Bahá'u'lláh. *Bahá'í World Faith: Selected Writings of Bahá'u'lláh and 'Abdu'l-Bahá*. Rev. ed. Wilmette, Illinois: Bahá'í Publishing Trust, 1956.

Adorno, T.W. *The Authoritarian Personality*. New York: Harper, 1950.

Allport, Gordon W. *The Person in Psychology: Selected Essays*. Boston: Beacon Press, 1968.

Bahá'u'lláh. *Gleanings from the Writings of Bahá'u'lláh*. Trans. Shoghi Effendi. 2d ed. Wilmette, Illinois: Bahá'í Publishing Trust, 1976.

_____. *The Seven Valleys and the Four Valleys*. Trans. Marzieh Gail. 3d ed. Wilmette, Illinois: Bahá'í Publishing Trust, 1978.

_____. *A Synopsis and Codification of the Laws and Ordinances of the Kitáb-i-Aqdas*. Comp. The Universal House of Justice. Haifa: Bahá'í World Centre, 1973.

_____. *Tablets of Bahá'u'lláh, Revealed after the Kitáb-i-Aqdas*. Haifa: Bahá'í World Centre, 1978.

Balyuzi, H.M. *'Abdu'l-Bahá*. Oxford: George Ronald, 1971.

Bettelheim, Bruno. *Surviving and Other Essays*. New York: Vintage Books, 1980.

Bronowski, Jacob. *The Ascent of Man*. Boston: Little, Brown and Co., 1973.

Brown, Dee. *Bury My Heart at Wounded Knee: An Indian History of the American West*. New York: Holt, Rinehart and Winston, 1970.

Capra, Fritjof. *The Turning Point: Science, Society, and the Rising Culture*. Toronto: Bantam Books, 1983.

Danesh, Hossain B. "The Violence-Free Society: A Gift for Our Children." 2d ed. *Bahá'í Studies*. Vol. 6(October 1979).

Eekelaar, John M. and Sanford N. Katz, eds. *Family Violence: An International and Interdisciplinary Study*. Toronto: Butterworth, 1978.

Bibliography

Einstein, Albert. *Out of My Later Years*. New York: Philosophical Library, 1950.

Freud, Sigmund. "Why War?" In *Complete Psychological Works*. Trans. J. Strachey. Standard Ed. London: Hogarth Press, 1964.

Fromm, Erich. *Escape from Freedom*. New York: Avon Books, 1969.

Gorney, Roderic. *The Human Agenda*. New York: Bantam Books, 1973.

Gregg, Richard B. *The Power of Nonviolence*. 2d ed. New York: Schocken Books, 1966.

Hofstadter, Douglas and Daniel C. Dennett, eds. *The Mind's I*. Toronto: Bantam Books, 1982.

Lasch, Christopher. *The Culture of Narcissism*. New York: W.W. Norton, 1978.

Laszlo, Ervin et al. *Goals for Mankind: A Report to the Club of Rome on the New Horizons of Global Community*. Foreword by Aurelio Peccei and Alexander King. New York: E.P. Dutton, 1977.

Leakey, Richard E. and Roger Lewin, *Origins: What New Discoveries Reveal about the Emergence of Our Species and its Possible Future*. New York: E.P. Dutton, 1977.

Lorenz, Konrad. *On Aggression*. Trans. Marjorie Latzke. London: Methuen and Co., 1966.

Martin, Douglas. "The Persecution of the Bahá'ís of Iran 1844-1984."*Bahá'í Studies*. Vol. 12/13(1984).

Matson, Floyd. *The Idea of Man*. New York: Delacorte Press, 1976.

May, Rollo. *Power and Innocence: A Search for the Sources of Violence*. New York: Delta Books, 1972.

Montagu, Ashley. *Man and Aggression*. New York: Oxford University Press, 1968.

Naisbitt, John. *Megatrends*. New York: Warner Books, 1984.

Peccei, Aurelio. "The Imperative of a New Humanism." In *Dilemmas of Modern Man*. Winnipeg, Canada: Great-West Life Assurance Company, 1975.

Pope, Kenneth S. et al., eds., *On Love and Loving*. San Francisco: Jossey-Bass Publishers, 1980.

Reshetovskaya, Natalya. *Sanya: My Husband Aleksandr Solzhenitsyn*. Trans. Elena Ivanoff. London: Hart-Davis, MacGibbon, 1975.

Sartre, Jean-Paul. *The Anti-Semite and Jew*. New York: Schocken Books, 1966.

Schaefer, Udo. *The Imperishable Dominion*. Trans. Janet Rawling-Keitel, David Hopper and Patricia Crampton. Oxford: George Ronald, 1983.

Shaw, George Bernard. *Man and Superman*. Vol. 10 of *The Collected Works of Bernard Shaw*. New York: Wm. H. Wise Company, 1930.

Shoghi Effendi. *The Advent of Divine Justice*. 3d ed. Wilmette, Illinois: Bahá'í Publishing Trust, 1969.

_____. *Principles of Bahá'í Administration*. 3d ed. London: Bahá'í Publishing Trust, 1973.

_____. *The Promised Day Is Come*. 3d ed. Wilmette, Illinois: Bahá'í Publishing Trust, 1980.

_____. *World Order of Bahá'u'lláh, Selected Letters*. 2d ed. Wilmette, Illinois: Bahá'í Publishing Trust, 1974.

Bibliography

Stanovnik, Janez. "The Debit Balance of the Mistakes of Several Decades." In
  What Kind of a World Are We Leaving Our Children? Paris: UNESCO, 1978.
Toffler, Alvin. *Future Shock*. New York: Bantam Books, 1971.
Tolstoy, Leo. *War and Peace*. Trans. Constance Garnett. New York: The Modern
  Library, 1931.
Toynbee, Arnold. *A Study of History*. New York: Oxford University Press, 1972.
Turner, Frederick. "Escape from Modernism." In *Harper's*. Nov. 1984.
Universal House of Justice. *Messages from the Universal House of Justice
  1968-1973*. Wilmette, Illinois: Bahá'í Publishing Trust, 1976.

Index

'Abdu'l-Bahá, 9, 12–13, 15, 21,
    22–23, 31, 35, 78, 80,
    87–88, 107, 116–117
Anarchy
    avoidance of, 105
    created by indulgent
        mode, 52
    in interpersonal relation-
        ships, 53
Anxiety, 8, 14, 18, 49, 62
Armaments, 9, 38, 40, 75, 78, 104
Atom, 31, 69, 73, 77
Audrey, R., 13
Auschwitz, 62
Authoritarian, 48–51
    approach to life, 50
    attitude of men, 50
Authoritarian mode, 48–50
    abuse of power, 50
    as a characteristic of
        childhood, 49–50
    avoidance of pain, 49
    coexistence with indulgent
        mode, 53
    contrasted with indulgent
        mode, 55
    contrasted with integrative
        mode, 54
    dichotomous perception, 50
    importance of obedience, 50
    inability to reach
        potential, 55
    major characteristics
        of, 49–51
    most common in human
        relationships, 48
    of government, 51
    relationship to power, 49
    rigidity in, 50
    roots of, 50
    schema of, 56
    stages of development, 48
    use of power, 55
Authoritarian personality
    avoids change, 51
    based on pursuit of
        power, 49
    characteristics of, 54
    dichotomous perception, 54
    link between love and
        power, 49
    unable to reach creative
        potential, 55

Authoritarian relationships
    demands of, 55
Authoritarian societies, 53
Authoritarian submission, 50, 56
Authoritarianism
    prevalent in democratic
        societies, 51
Autonomy, 114

Báb, the, 103–104
Bábí, 103–105, 107
Bahá'í
    approach to human
        violence, 105
    community in Iran, 100,
        102–103, 109
    concept of liberty, 64–65
    perspective of peace, 86
    response to
        violence, 108–109
    spiritual concept of
        man, 70–71
    view of religion, 35
Bahá'í Faith, 108
    history of, 103–104
    response to
        violence, 108–109
Bahá'u'lláh, 24–26, 34, 37, 39, 41,
    67–68, 74, 99, 104–106
Balyuzi, H.M., 40
Behaviour
    adoption of new types, 45
    destructive forms of, 14
    aggressive, 93, 99
Bettelheim, B., 62, 65
Bronowski, J., 37, 80
Browne, E.G., 76
Brutality, 65, 73, 94, 108–109
Burton, R., 14

Capitalism, 35
Capra, F., 10, 19, 78, 112–113
Character, 49
Civilization, 18–19, 21, 45, 51–52,
    62, 67, 69, 79, 89, 99, 102,
    105, 112–114, 122
Club of Rome, 5, 19, 33, 68
Cobb, Stanwood, 11
Coming of age, 81, 86, 89, 112, 121
Communism, 36
Copernican revolution, 62, 65
Counterviolence, 94
Creation, 24, 50, 54, 62, 64, 66,

70, 80
    of a technology of peace, 121
    of a united global
        society, 121
Crime, 12
Cruelty, 10, 74, 99, 103
Culture, 33, 52, 68, 70

Dart, R., 13
Darwinian revolution, 62, 65
Davies, P., 73
Deak, F., 94
Death, 3, 4, 15, 19, 62, 72, 76, 93,
    98, 101–103
Deeds, 33, 102, 105–106
Democracy, 36, 51, 92, 112
Despair, 7, 41, 79, 91
Dignity, 67–68
Discipline, 52–53, 55, 66, 95
Disease, 10, 14, 25, 39, 59, 72, 91,
    93, 96, 97, 115
Disorder, 34, 37, 52, 75
    economic, 18
Distrust, 8, 38, 97
Disunity, 11, 12, 25, 51, 57, 63, 79,
    86, 88–89, 96–97, 105, 111
Divine, 71, 73–74, 80
    compassion, 71
Divine Physician, 40
Domination, 10, 14, 89
    of man over woman, 43, 45
    of spiritual qualities, 112
Drinkwater, J., 42
Drives
    animalistic, 33
    animalistic, freedom from
        rule of, 66–67
    for cooperation, 88
    sexual, 15
Earth, 40, 61–62, 63, 68, 86, 87
    as the centre of the
        universe, 61–62
Economic
    barriers, abolished, 115
    causes of war, 10–11
    disorder, 18
    ideologies, contribution to
        injustice, 10
    interdependence, 32
    resources of the world, 115
    rivalry between nations, 10
    structure, need for a new
        one, 112

131